Energy Politics and Disc(in Canada

This book examines the discourse around the intricate economic, political, and ideological struggles underlying Canadian fuel extractivism. Focusing on the two contending discourse coalitions formed by supporters and opponents of British Columbia's liquefied natural gas (LNC) industry, the book explores the ongoing debates around the issue.

The book's in-depth investigation of the BC LNG controversy identifies progressive extractivism as an increasingly popular policy/discursive paradigm adopted by fossil fuel advocates to legitimize unconventional fossil fuels in an era of intensifying climate crisis. It also highlights the importance of debunking the misleading "jobs versus the environment" dichotomy in mobilizing public opposition to carbon-intensive economic growth.

This deeply nuanced look at energy discourse in public policy will have resonance for scholars and students working in the areas of environmental communication, rhetoric, discourse analysis, public policy, and climate change rhetoric.

Sibo Chen is Assistant Professor at the School of Professional Communication, Toronto Metropolitan University, Canada. He is also an executive board member of International Environmental Communication Association (2021–2025). His current research explores how political polarization is communicated in the public sphere, focusing on three topics: political contention over climate change, online mis/disinformation, and the rise of anti-Asian racism.

Routledge Focus on Communication Studies

For more information about this series, please visit: www.routledge.com

Energy Politics and Discourse in Canada

in Canada

Probing Progressive Extractivism

Sibo Chen

Routledge
Taylor & Francis Group

LONDON AND NEW YORK

First published 2024
by Routledge
4 Park Square, Milton Park, Abingdon, Oxon OX14 4RN

and by Routledge
605 Third Avenue, New York, NY 10158

Routledge is an imprint of the Taylor & Francis Group, an informa business

British Library Cataloguing-in-Publication Data
A catalogue record for this book is available from the British Library

ISBN: 978-1-032-39552-4 (hbk)
ISBN: 978-1-032-39630-9 (pbk)
ISBN: 978-1-003-35062-0 (ebk)

DOI: 10.4324/9781003350620

Typeset in Times New Roman
by Apex CoVantage, LLC

Contents

1   Introduction

This book originates from my curiosity about the continued dominance of extractivism in Canada's political economy. In 2015, I first learned about the public disputes surrounding British Columbia's (BC) ambition of establishing a liquefied natural gas (LNG) industry targeting Asian markets. Back then, the provincial Liberal government aggressively promoted LNG as a clean alternative to coal and framed its export as a significant contribution to reducing greenhouse gas (GHG) emissions and improving the air quality of developing nations like China and India. Echoing such branding of natural gas as a "bridge fuel", domestic proponents of fossil fuels made similar claims advertising LNG as the optimal solution for maintaining global economic growth in the upcoming era of climate emergency. I was intrigued by the inherent contradiction in such claims: to address problems caused by GHG emissions, why not develop policies that facilitate a direct transition to renewable energy sources? How could the creation of a brand-new fossil fuel industry be considered a viable climate solution?

My knowledge of environmental communication convinced me that the LNG boosterism of the BC Liberal government and industry stakeholders must conceal something worthy of further investigation. This eventually led me to analyse "LNG in British Columbia" (https://lnginbc.gov.bc.ca/), the website showcasing the official development blueprint of BC LNG. My analysis (Chen & Gunster, 2016) found that the website's discourse concerning LNG's environmental benefits relies heavily on accentuating the ethereal characteristics of natural gas in contrast to the material density and toxicity of other fossil fuels like coal and bitumen. Constructing this conceptual binary enables the BC Liberal government to brand LNG as an ethical choice deserving the support of environmentally minded British Columbians.

Inspired by this study, my research on Canadian energy politics continued. The BC Liberal government is not alone in pursuing resource-based prosperity. Since the 2000s, other Canadian provinces have implemented similar policy initiatives with the hope of expanding their resource industries. While Alberta has actively defended its bitumen industry against public doubts brought by growing environmental concerns and global market volatility,

DOI: 10.4324/9781003350620-1

Atlantic provinces (New Brunswick, Nova Scotia, and Newfoundland and Labrador) have explored various ways to further develop their offshore drilling and shale gas production. When I read about such energy initiatives in the news, I often wondered what factors make resource extraction such a default choice for Canadian policymakers. What has kept appearing in related public discussions is a taken-for-granted attitude towards maintaining Canada as a resource hinterland. As someone born in Mainland China, I still remember how my high school political courses kept emphasizing the necessity of shielding the national economy and politics from foreign interference, yet what I have witnessed in Canadian policymaking and public discourse is in sharp contrast to this Chinese belief.

The pursuit of developing LNG exports as an economic engine by the BC Liberal government proved to be a fad that lasted only six years (late 2011 to mid-2017). Was this failure caused by changing Asian energy market conditions, by strong political resistance on the ground, or by other factors? In addition, what does this case tell us about the relationship between the business risks associated with LNG exports and the environmental concerns associated with fracking during shale gas production? Compared with the existing communication scholarship on Alberta's bitumen industry, the case of BC LNG presents a less studied but equally important public controversy for empirical research. During the heyday of the LNG craze, the BC Liberal government actively promoted a progressive approach to resource extraction by framing LNG exports as a major component of its environmental leadership. This promotional strategy has gained prominence in Canadian energy politics, as evidenced by the federal government's attempt to implement GHG reduction measures without harming the short-term interests of the oil and gas industry (Chun, 2021 November 15). In this regard, the not-so-distant past of BC LNG presents an excellent case for examining the ongoing political contests over extractivism in Canada.

1.1. Why Study Public Debates over LNG in British Columbia?

In the inaugural issue of *Environmental Communication*, Robert Cox (2007) wrote that

> the field of environmental communication arises at a moment of conjunctural crisis, defined in not insignificant ways by human-caused threats to both biological systems and human communities, and also by the continuing failure of societal institutions to sufficiently engage these pressures.
>
> (p. 7)

Inspired by Cox's definition of environmental communication as a crisis-driven discipline, this book asserts itself not as a purely academic work but as a critical intervention in Canada's intensifying political struggles over extractive industries. I intend to provide both an analysis and a critique of how stakeholders and the news media communicate about BC LNG, based on the premises that (1) climate change mitigation requires radical policy measures addressing contemporary society's addiction to fossil fuels, and (2) public communication plays an essential role in the global pursuit of a sustainable future.

The heated public debates sparked by the development of LNG projects in British Columbia reveal the complexity of Canadian energy politics. As a contested policy issue, BC LNG is located at the intersection of economic, social, political, and environmental concerns, and its shifting meaning "enables cooperation and contestation between different social worlds, such as science, policy, and society" (Metze, 2017, p. 37). Between September 2011 and August 2017, a wide range of stakeholders employed multiple discursive frames to contest the meaning of LNG and knowledge about it in the BC public sphere. From these contests came two competing "storylines" (Hajer, 1995; Dryzek, 2013) that shaped public understandings of LNG policies. Thus, an in-depth study of the public discourses surrounding BC LNG has important theoretical implications for comprehending how the discursive dynamics of competing stakeholders drive the evolvement of a policy controversy.

From a political economy perspective, the concerted efforts of the BC Liberal government and its industry allies to expand domestic shale gas extraction and establish LNG exports to Asia reflect the rise of transnational carbon capitalism. The rapid expansion of unconventional fossil fuel production has profoundly reshaped Canadian capitalism and society as the 21st century unfolds (Pineault, 2018). As Canada's gateway to Asian energy markets, British Columbia has been a key battleground between extractive capital and its opponents. Over the past two decades, the province has witnessed intense political struggles over several mega energy projects, such as the Enbridge Northern Gateway Pipeline and the Trans Mountain Pipeline Expansion. Both projects were designed to increase Canada's fossil fuel industry's export capacity to Asia. To the Canadian fossil fuel industry, Asia's fast-growing energy consumption presents an irresistible destination for a treasure hunt.

Meanwhile, mainstream narratives in the Canadian public sphere have exhibited a laissez-faire attitude towards extractivism and neoliberal globalization. In my analysis of the "LNG in British Columbia" website, I criticized its rhetorical simplification of the political economy of Asian energy markets. In hindsight, the mythification of Asia is symptomatic of the Canadian economy's continuous dependence on staple extraction. Among policymakers, this has constructed a "dependency mindset", which, as a complex discursive framework, justifies Canada's continued status as a hinterland of other industrial economies (Neubauer, 2018; Veltmeyer & Bowles, 2014). Although sociology and political economy have offered extensive discussions on this mindset, communication research on it remains scarce (Gunster et al., 2018), which adds importance to the current study of BC LNG.

The controversial LNG policies in British Columbia were also closely tied to the recent surge of unconventional fossil fuel production in North America and globally (Davidson & Gismondi, 2011; Fast, 2014; Pineault, 2018). British Columbia has abundant natural gas reserves located in its northeast interior, which is home to many small towns and First Nations communities (BC Ministry of Natural Gas Development, 2013). For decades, the production and trade of BC gas were relatively stable since it was extracted primarily for domestic consumption and exported merely to Alberta and adjacent US states.

Since the mid-2000s, however, structural changes have fundamentally altered the BC gas industry's decades-long business model (Gomes, 2015). Following the US shale gas boom, innovations in extraction technologies (especially horizontal drilling and hydraulic fracturing) have dramatically boosted the estimation of British Columbia's technically recoverable natural gas reserves (BC Ministry of Natural Gas Development, 2013). As a result of booming domestic production, the North American market has been experiencing a prolonged price decline since 2008. By contrast, economic growth in Asia during the same period has prompted regional natural gas prices to rise. In this context, LNG exports from North America to Asia have become an attractive proposition for energy investors as well as policymakers. In British Columbia, the state-industry alliance's pursuit of LNG exports constellated into LNG project proposals, pro-LNG policies, and promotional discourses during the 2011–2017 period.

Nonetheless, developing an export-oriented LNG industry in British Columbia is a complicated task requiring three key components (Gomes, 2015). To begin, the scale of natural gas extraction in the province must be dramatically enlarged to supply the large volumes of gas needed to justify building mega LNG facilities. This inevitably involves a substantial increase in fracking, the colloquial term describing the combination of horizontal drilling and hydraulic fracturing. This unconventional fossil fuel extraction method has proven controversial during the US shale gas boom, drawing growing scholarly attention (e.g., Matthews & Hansen, 2018; Wylie, 2018) to its social and ecological impacts. In their assessment of regional effects of proposed shale gas development in Fort Nelson (a community in northeast British Columbia), Garvie and her colleagues (2014) warned that if the development proceeded as planned, it would threaten local wildlife habitats, significantly increase water use and the risk of underground water contamination and have negative impacts on local air quality and global GHG emissions.

Given fracking's central role in many environmental controversies across the world, this book is intended to contribute to the research on its public communication. Compared with fracking controversies elsewhere, the case of BC LNG includes additional factors meriting scholarly attention. To transport large volumes of gas to coastal LNG facilities for liquefaction and export, the province must upgrade its current gas pipeline network. This task involves extensive negotiations with different stakeholders, and disagreement could escalate into heightened political tension. For instance, since 2015, activists from the Wet'suwet'en First Nation have taken a series of actions, including setting up roadblocks and check points, to oppose a gas pipeline being built across their traditional territory (Jeong, 2019 January 8).

Additionally, LNG facilities must be constructed near coastal BC communities for gas liquefaction and marine transport, threatening the ecology and living environment of these communities. Not only are these facilities highly capital intensive, but the process of liquefaction consumes large quantities of electricity, which, if produced through gas-powered plants, generates considerable GHG emissions.

In anticipation of this challenge, the BC Liberal government announced in 2010 that it would construct a mega hydroelectric dam (the Site C project) on the Peace River. This would enable renewable energy sources to meet the anticipated electricity consumption from gas liquefaction. However, the adverse environmental impacts of Site C soon turned it into a public controversy of its own (Eagle, 2017 March 23).

Besides the multiple components required for establishing the LNG industry, the strong environmental sentiment among the BC public presents another barrier for the legitimization of extractive projects. British Columbia has a long tradition of environmental activism. In the 1980s, Clayoquot Sound on Vancouver Island witnessed the War in the Woods, a series of protests that included the largest number of arrests for civil disobedience in Canadian history (Wilson, 1999). More recently, public mobilization for environmental causes re-emerged during the BC public's strong opposition to the Northern Gateway Pipeline Project and the Trans Mountain Pipeline Expansion (Hackett & Adams, 2018; Neubauer, 2018). Additionally, BC First Nations are highly politically active: few treaties were signed during colonization, which means that most of the province is subject to aboriginal title, giving First Nations legal and political leverage to resist development initiatives imposed by government and industry. Last but not least, British Columbia became the first jurisdiction in North America to implement a comprehensive carbon tax in 2007–2008 and subsequently committed to significant GHG emissions reduction. As such, the BC Liberal government's promotion of LNG stands in stark contrast to its oft-proclaimed progressive stance on tackling climate change.

Another notable feature of the arguments made by critics of BC LNG projects was that they had problematized LNG exports through a number of economic analyses, which complicated the conventional "jobs versus the environment" dichotomy typically present environmental politics (Hackett & Adams, 2018). This dichotomy, according to Matthews and Hansen's (2018) review of research on fracking controversies in the US and Europe, has emerged as a prevalent pattern denoting polarized contests between stakeholders regarding resource extraction as an economic good and those regarding it as an environmental threat.

In British Columbia, however, the uncertainty of the business case for LNG exports has sparked criticism of their economic grounds. Each LNG facility will be a multi-billion investment requiring both a steady supply of gas from the BC interior and long-term contracts with Asian buyers. Yet, securing these long-term contracts will be difficult due to the volatility of the global gas commodity landscape (Lee, 2014). After all, countries like China, South Korea, and Japan have little reason to lock themselves into using BC gas when they could get similar supplies from the expanding Eurasian natural gas system and growing shipments from other LNG exporters like Qatar, Australia, Malaysia, and Indonesia. Accordingly, some have suggested that the economic case for LNG exports depends upon the province offering significant concessions and subsidies, which weakens the economic good rhetoric. For example, Graham's (2017) analysis of political donations and corporate lobbying accompanying BC LNG's policy planning process made the case that the fossil fuel industry was exercising undue influence upon the formation of BC energy policies, including favourable treatment with respect to land access, corporate taxation, and royalty rates from shale gas extraction, amongst other issues.

In sum, the case of BC LNG presents an extractivist endeavor suffering from a multitude of challenges. Despite these obstacles, the BC Liberal government still chose to bet the province's economic future on LNG exports. Between late 2011 and mid-2017, it devoted considerable effort into promoting the business case for LNG exports to the public and potential investors. What factors made it so addictive to resource-based development, and how did environmental organizations and their allies fight back? To answer these questions, this book analyzes the discursive contests between LNG proponents and opponents.

1.2. Case Study: British Columbia's Pursuit of LNG Exports from Late 2011 to Mid-2017

To contextualize the follow chapter's discussion of the BC LNG controversy, this section briefly reviews its major milestones between late 2011 and mid-2017, which informed relevant public debates. The BC Liberal government's ambition of LNG development first entered public view with the release of *Canada Starts Here: The BC Jobs Plan* (BC Office of the Premier, 2011 October 26). This policy document envisioned the creation of a prosperous LNG export sector as a key strategy for the province's future job growth. Then in February 2012, the BC Liberal government's pro-LNG efforts consolidated into a development blueprint (BC Ministry of Energy and Mines, 2012 February 03a) in which LNG was branded as "the cleanest fossil fuel in the world", which would simultaneously deliver economic prosperity and strengthen British Columbia's environmental leadership. In many respects, the blueprint's language resembles Alberta's approach to bitumen development in the 1990s, particularly its emphasis on attracting private investment in LNG infrastructure by removing policy barriers and lowering taxation, as opposed to stimulating sectoral development through publicly funded projects. Shortly after releasing the blueprint, the BC Liberal government launched the "LNG in British Columbia" website, which functioned as the primary information portal promoting British Columbia's LNG policies in subsequent years.

By the end of 2012, it became evident that the business interests in LNG exports, with help from the governing BC Liberal Party's tirelessly promotional efforts, had grown from several individual project proposals into a comprehensive economic blueprint that would dominate the provincial public agenda in upcoming years. During this period, three major proposals worth billions of dollars sparked the public's imagination regarding "LNG prosperity": the Pacific NorthWest LNG (PNW) project proposed by a consortium led by Malaysian oil and gas conglomerates Petronas, the LNG Canada project by a Shell-led consortium, and the Kitimat LNG project by Chevron and Woodside Petroleum.

The 40th BC general election took place in May 2013, and the BC Liberal Party made LNG the central topic of this election as a means of salvaging their electoral fortunes with a public which had grown tired of the Liberal Party's governance. Three months before the election, the then governing Christy Clark administration announced the BC Prosperity Fund, a savings fund to be supported by LNG revenues. Considering the timing of this announcement, it was widely recognized a campaign message to swing voters that the BC Liberal Party had chosen LNG as their primary economic platform. In follow-up statements concerning the provincial election, Christy Clark even touted the idea that once LNG exports to Asia took off, BC would be debt-free over the next decade. The BC Liberal Party won the provincial election with majority status and consequently had economic promises to fulfil.

Along with the advancement of the BC Liberal Party's LNG agenda, the PNW project gradually became the flagship proposal due to its enormous amount of investment. In June 2013, Petronas, the project's primary industry stakeholder, announced up to $16 billion spending on it ("Petronas to spend up to $16B on BC LNG project", 2013 June 11), which the BC Liberal government framed as a strong indicator of the LNG boom. Six months later, the National Energy Board approved PNW, along with three other LNG proposals.

In February 2014, the BC Liberal government introduced two-tiered LNG royalty rates in its annual budget: 1.5% at the start of an LNG facility's production and a later increase to 7% after all the capital costs of construction have been recouped through sales. In response, industry stakeholders deemed both rates as unacceptable. Later in September, for instance, Petronas's CEO, Shamsul Abbas, threatened to cancel PNW, arguing that "rather than ensuring the development of the LNG industry through appropriate incentives and assurance of legal and fiscal stability, the Canadian landscape of LNG development is now one of uncertainty, delay and short vision" ("Petronas may pull out of BC LNG project", 2014 September 25, para. 3).

The pushback from Petronas and other industry stakeholders emerged along with a plunge in Asian natural gas prices. After fluctuating around high price points between mid-2011 and mid-2014, Asian LNG prices dropped considerably. In subsequent years, the narrowing price gap between North America's benchmark and Asia's benchmark substantially diminished the trans-Pacific LNG trade's profit margin. The BC Liberal government, feeling the pressure of corporate capital threatening to abandon LNG development, conceded and offered tax breaks to the PNW project, which persuaded Petronas to make a preliminary investment decision in June 2015. In the decision, Petronas stated that the project would proceed if it satisfied two conditions: approval of a project development agreement by the BC legislature and clearing of the federal environmental assessment review process.

The year 2016 began with two blows to the BC LNG agenda. In early February, Shell announced that it would delay the final investment decision on the LNG Canada project until the end of 2016 since it was hit by a 44% slump in earnings due to low oil prices (Hussain, 2016 February 5). Only two weeks after Shell's announcement, AltaGas canceled its Douglas Channel project, attributing the decision to poor economic conditions and worsening global energy prices ("BC LNG: AltaGas shelves Douglas Channel project near Kitimat", 2016 February 25). Notwithstanding these negative developments, the newly elected federal Liberal government still approved PNW in September 2016, with 190 conditions covering issues from human health concerns to GHG emissions (Tasker, 2016 September 27).

Asian natural gas prices rebounded only slightly at the beginning of 2017, which further clouded the economic prospect of proposed BC LNG projects. In March 2017, Shell cancelled the Prince Rupert LNG project, which it inherited from its 2016 acquisition of British natural gas company BG Group. With another provincial election coming in May, the BC Liberal Party downplayed the economic promises they had made four years ago. In a fact check published one month before the election, CBC journalists Rankin and McElroy (2017 April 11) reviewed the progress of BC LNG from 2012 to 2017 and concluded that this mega-promise was not an achievable plan.

During the 41st BC general election, the three major provincial parties showed very different attitudes towards LNG. The Liberal Party remained optimistic about the BC LNG industry's outlook, though they carefully avoided questions about when LNG exports would actually begin. The New Democratic Party (NDP) criticized the Liberals' handling of negotiations with industry stakeholders but also insisted that it would support LNG projects considering job creation in rural communities. The Greens strongly opposed LNG and called for a total ban on fracking. The election resulted in the NDP forming a minority government with the support of the Greens.

Shortly after the new government took office, Petronas officially cancelled PNW in July 2017. Although Petronas attributed the cancellation to changes in market conditions and maintained that provincial politics did not influence its decision (Ghoussou, 2017 July 25), BC Liberal politicians and other LNG proponents quickly linked it to the likelihood that the new provincial government would introduce development-killing environmental regulations and high taxes. The death of PNW was a significant setback for the BC LNG agenda. Nonetheless, the NDP minority government reaffirmed its support for the LNG industry, and in 2018, it secured a favorable investment decision for the LNG Canada project, which received investments from companies including Shell and Petronas that had canceled other BC LNG project proposals. After multiple delays, the project's construction remains incomplete in 2023, and the vision of establishing the LNG industry as a major economic sector for British Columbia has faded away from public discourse.

1.3. Research Methods

This book provides an in-depth examination of how the social meanings of shale gas shifted during 2011–2017, when the BC LNG controversy garnered sustained public attention. For this purpose, it empirically analyzes how notable stakeholders constructed multiple public narratives of BC LNG, as shown in their primary communication materials, such as government documents, research reports, news opinion pieces, and blog posts. It also critically assesses how the major disputes between LNG proponents and opponents led to the formation of two competing discourse coalition (i.e., pro-LNG versus anti-LNG) and their respective storylines that influenced media coverage. Based on the empirical findings, I further elaborate on the BC LNG controversy's implications for understanding the economic, political, and ideological tensions underlying global capitalism's embrace of unconventional fossil fuels.

The primary methodological framework guiding the empirical analysis is the argumentative discourse analysis (ADA) approach developed by Maarten Hajer (1995, 2005). According to this constructivist approach, argumentative interaction is a relatively independent layer of power practices. Members of a discourse coalition, such as the one supporting the development of an LNG industry in British Columbia, are united by similar interpretations of policy issues. Scholars following ADA define such policy interpretations as "storylines" that, by integrating facts and normative orientations into persuasive narrative structures, constantly influence policy debates through symbolic means (Dryzek, 2013; Metze & Dodge, 2016). Climate change skepticism, for instance, is often delivered through conspiratorial stories that attack scientists, green activists, and environmental groups.

Storylines tend to be metaphorical to offer "cognitive shortcuts" for public discussions. In Hajer's (1995, 2005) analysis of the acid rain controversy in Northern Europe during the 1980s, for instance, the term "acid rain" itself is a metaphor that connects the meteorological phenomenon of "acid precipitation" to the public's general fear of acid corrosion. Acid precipitation affects ecosystems in complex ways, not as simply as pouring acid on trees, yet the powerful symbolic connotations of "acid rain" make it an attention-grabbing issue for policy makers and citizens. Thus, stakeholder coalitions during policy deliberation are in fact discourse coalitions. Members belonging to the same discourse coalition may not meet each other in person, but their activities collectively perpetuate and reinforce a set of storylines concerning a particular policy domain. The power of storylines lies in their ability to "offer social orientation, reassurance, or guidance", and "what people in an environmental discourse coalition support is an interpretation of threat or crisis, not a core set of facts and values that can be teased out through content or factor analysis" (Fischer, 2003, p. 103).

The collection of BC LNG-related public texts began by identifying the controversy's major stakeholders. After trying various methods, I decided to accomplish this step by browsing articles mentioning either "liquefied natural gas" or "LNG" in two websites: BC Government News (https://news.gov.bc.ca/) and Canada's public broadcaster CBC News (www.cbc.ca/news). When reading both websites, I took notes on specific stakeholders mentioned in their articles. The initial overview identified a total of 26 notable stakeholders (Table 1.1). I also drew from my personal observation of the BC LNG controversy since 2016 (Chen & Gunster, 2016) to confirm these stakeholders' active participation in public debates over LNG. These stakeholders could be categorized as belonging to either pro- or anti-LNG coalitions according to their stances on LNG development. It should be acknowledged that discourse coalitions tend to be fluid and context-sensitive, and there can be a shift in actors and institutions within and between storylines.

The pro-LNG coalition was led by the BC Liberal government and its politicians. For industry stakeholders, I focused on the energy corporations behind three LNG proposals: PNW, LNG Canada, and Woodfibre LNG – because they were the most frequently discussed ones in CBC's news coverage. These corporations' interests were advanced by domestic and international fossil fuel advocates. Although some of these advocates came from industry associations (e.g., the BC LNG Alliance) and pro-industry policy institutes (e.g., the Fraser Institute), there were also settler and Indigenous civil groups supporting the LNG agenda.

The anti-LNG coalition, in contrast, was a spontaneous formation with no discernible leadership. It mainly consisted of environmental organizations, progressive policy institutes, concerned citizens, some Indigenous communities, and independent media. Among them, the three most prominent members were the Canadian Centre for Policy Alternatives, the *Tyee*, and the *Common Sense Canadian*. Independent media were treated as part of the coalition because they not only frequently published critiques on BC LNG policies but also functioned as communication channels among LNG opponents.

Table 1.1 Notable Members of Pro- and Anti-LNG Coalitions

Discourse Coalitions	*Member Types*	*Notable Members*
Pro-LNG	BC Liberal government and its politicians	▪ BC Liberal government and its key "LNG champions", notably Christy Clarke, Rich Coleman, and Mike de Jong
	Industry associations	▪ International Gas Union ▪ Canadian Association of Petroleum Producers ▪ BC LNG Alliance
	Oil and gas corporations (as represented by major LNG project proposals)	▪ Pacific Northwest LNG (joint venture led by Petronas, with Sinopec, JAPEX, Indian Oil Corporation, and Petroleum BRUNEI as minority stakeholders) ▪ LNG Canada (joint venture by Shell, Petro-China, Mitsubishi, and Korea Gas; Petronas joined in 2018) ▪ Woodfibre LNG (Royal Golden Eagle as major investor)
	Pro-business policy institutes	▪ Fraser Institute ▪ Canadian Energy Research Institute ▪ Asia Pacific Foundation Canada ▪ Resource Works
	Grassroots supporters, including some Indigenous communities	▪ First Nations LNG Alliance ▪ Fort St. John for LNG
Anti-LNG	Environmental NGOs	▪ The Council of Canadians ▪ David Suzuki Foundation ▪ Sierra Club BC
	Progressive policy institutes	▪ Canadian Centre for Policy Alternatives ▪ Pembina Institute
	Grassroots opponents, including local residences and (some)	▪ Dogwood Initiative ▪ Union of BC Indian Chiefs ▪ Friends of Wild Salmon (led by the Lax Kw'alaams First Nation)
	Indigenous communities Independent media	▪ My Sea to Sky ▪ *Tyee* ▪ National Observer ▪ DeSmog Canada ▪ Common Sense Canadian

Following the identification of these stakeholders, I checked their home pages to collect publicly available communication materials and understand each one's specific viewpoints on BC LNG. The analysis of stakeholder communications aimed to identify important sources that larger being cited by mainstream media to set up BC LNG's news agenda. Based on initial reading of relevant CBC news stories, the manual search process targeted items containing any of the following keywords: "LNG", "natural gas", "shale gas", "hydraulic fracturing", and "fracking". More than 4,000 texts in various forms (press releases, public statements, research reports, blog posts, infographics, etc.) were collected. Considering the enormous quantity and the heterogeneous formats of these items, they were qualitatively analyzed following ADA's procedural guideline.

ADA emphasizes uncovering macro-argumentative features across multiple texts and the ways in which these features subsequently influence the contours of discursive coalitions and their respective storylines. Accordingly, the data analysis took the following steps. I began by reviewing the collected texts to identify major points of contention between LNG advocates and opponents. The interpretative nature of this step required comprehensive tracing of key ideas through multiple texts, which involved both wide and deep reading. For each stakeholder, I spent considerable time immersing myself in the details of its arguments, searching for clues to assess their tenor and nuance. Each collected item was interpreted in terms of its definition of LNG, its depiction of principal stakeholders and issues in LNG development, and proposed policy actions.

After considerable trial and error, themes began to emerge. In consultation with previous studies' analytical frameworks (especially Bomberg, 2017; Dodge & Lee, 2017; Olive & Delshad, 2017), my examination centered around eight key discursive frames, as listed in Table 1.2. Notably, both storylines deviated from the traditional "jobs versus the environment" dichotomy. LNG proponents expended extensive efforts to brand BC LNG as a clean energy that would make unique contributions to climate change mitigation. Meanwhile, LNG opponents drew on business risk analysis to deem BC LNG an economic sham born of an extractivist state's collusion with fossil fuel lobbyists.

Following the identification of both storylines, I then assessed their strengths and weaknesses according to the criteria of plausibility, relevance, and trustworthiness (Table 1.3). According to Bomberg (2017), a compelling storyline must be backed up with plausible evidence, resonate with recipients'

Table 1.2 List of Key Discursive Frames

Storylines	Discursive Frames
Pro-LNG: Prosperity, environmental stewardship, and global competitiveness	▪ Economic opportunities ▪ Bridge fuel and environmental stewardship ▪ The dilemma of competitiveness ▪ Reviving rural BC and reconciling with First Nations via resource-driven development
Anti-LNG: Environmental threat, economic sham, and political corruption	▪ Environmental and health risks ▪ Questionable economic prospects and fossil fuel "lock-in" ▪ The formation of "extractivist state" and bad governance ▪ Indigenous-led resistance to LNG

Table 1.3 Storyline Assessment Criteria

- Plausibility: Whether a storyline is backed up by compelling scientific, moral, or affective reasons
- Relevance: Whether a storyline's claims appear applicable to recipients' everyday experiences
- Trustworthiness: Whether a storyline's sources are seen by recipients as reliable

Adapted from Bomberg (2017) and Hajer (1995)

daily lives, and come from trustworthy sources. The three criteria could be a storyline's potential strength as well as vulnerability.

To further evaluate the extent to which each storyline influenced Canadian media coverage of the BC LNG controversy, I also conducted a follow-up study comparing public, commercial, and independent media coverage of PNW, whose cancellation in 2017 marked a major turning point of the BC LNG agenda. Table 1.4 summarizes the basic information of the six media outlets analyzed: CBC News, the *Globe and Mail*, the *National Post*, the *Vancouver Sun*, the *Tyee*, and *Canada's National Observer*. In terms of data collection, I used "Petronas" and "Pacific NorthWest LNG" as search terms in Factiva to collect relevant news items published by the target media between September 2014 and August 2017. September 2014 is chosen as the starting point of data collection because back then Petronas issued its initial threat of withdrawing the PNW proposal, which publicized the deep disagreement between the BC government and the Petronas-led consortium and prompted media speculation over the outlook of BC LNG.

Because the web publications of CBC News, the *Tyee*, and *Canada's National Observer* were not indexed in Factiva at the time of data collection, I manually searched their websites to collect the relevant news items. The Factiva search found nearly 30% of identical news items shared by the *National Post* and the *Vancouver Sun*, which was unsurprising considering Postmedia Network owns both titles. To avoid repetition, their news items were treated as one media source under the "Postmedia" label. A total of 618 news items were collected, including 67 from CBC News, 196 from the *Globe and Mail*, 284 from Postmedia, 44 from the *Tyee*, and 27 from *Canada's National Observer*.

The comparative media study began with a quantitative content analysis. I carefully read and coded each news item for its manifest theme, as determined by its title and beginning paragraphs. I conducted a trial coding of the CBC News items to identify news themes that received sustained media attention. The themes fall into three categories and provide a snapshot of the perspectives from which issues related to PNW were reported to the public (Table 1.5). The patterns revealed by the quantitative content analysis revealed three issues that received recurring discussions in the data: (1) the challenges of starting an LNG export sector in BC from scratch, (2) the political implications of divided grassroots responses to PNW LNG, and (3) the contradiction

Table 1.4 Profiles of Target Media Outlets

Name	Type	Profile
CBC News	Public	CBC News is the web portal of Canada's national public broadcaster. As a public media institution, CBC gives high priority to accurate, objective, and impartial reporting. Its content thus focuses on providing factual information rather than siding with a particular camp during political controversies. Besides archiving and providing online access to CBC's television and radio programs, CBC News also publishes original news stories, which are the focus of the current analysis.
Globe and Mail	Commercial	The *Globe and Mail* is the most read national English daily in Canada. In 2018, the title reported a weekly combined digital and print readership of 6.5 million (Roy, 2018, January 25). According to Olive's (2016) analysis of Canadian media coverage on fracking, the *Globe and Mail* provides a relatively balanced reporting on the conflicts between the oil and gas sector and environmentalists.
National Post	Commercial	The *National Post* is Postmedia's flagship national daily that is in a rivalry with the *Globe and Mail*. A 2016 report estimated its weekly combined digital and print readership as 4.5 million ("National Post boosts weekly print and digital readership", 2016, July 26). Postmedia is known for its pro-business stance and close tie to the oil and gas sector (see Gunster & Saurette, 2014).
Vancouver Sun	Commercial	The *Vancouver Sun*, as the most circulated daily in Metro Vancouver, offers a glimpse into British Columbia's regional opinions. In 2016, its combined digital and print readership was estimated as 1.1 million ("Postmedia tops Canadian newspaper groups with highest readership", 2016 July 26). After being acquired by Postmedia in 2015, it has gradually turned into a center-right title keeping step with media conglomerate's pro-industry stance.
Tyee	Independent	Founded in 2003, the *Tyee* is a progressive online news magazine covering both local and national public affairs. It is amongst the most well established of Canadian independent media. The *Tyee* departs from commercial media's business model by rejecting advertising revenue from big corporations. It also makes explicit commitments to participatory and democratic forms of journalism. In 2017, the website reported an average of 300,000 to 400,000 unique visitors per month.
Canada's National Observer	Independent	Like the *Tyee*, the digital news site *Canada's National Observer* takes a negative stance on advertising revenue and is funded almost entirely by subscriptions. As described in a feature story by Nieman Lab (Owen, 2018 January 17), the site "covers issues like government, the environment, health, climate change, and human rights, all with a progressive bent" (para. 3). Founded in 2015, the site is a young contender in the Canadian media landscape, but several prestigious journalistic awards have helped it become a notable voice in public debates about Canadian environmental and energy politics. The website claims that it has reached nearly 7 million people since its inception in May 2015.

Table 1.5 Coding Scheme of News Sample

Economics
1.1. Negotiation: Business negotiations over LNG taxation and other policy
    incentives
1.2. Economic Development: PNW's economic benefits to the province
1.3. Project Uncertainty: Challenges to the project's viability
Politics
2.1. Public Opinion: Settler and Indigenous groups' responses to PNW news
2.2. Disputes from Opposition Parties: B.C. NDP and Green's views on PNW
2.3. Extractivist Policy Failure: Progressive critiques of extractivism and
2.4. Conservative Attacks: Conservative critiques of regulation and environmentalism
Environment
3.1. Review and Regulation: Government agencies' management of PNW related
    environmental risks
3.2. Alarming Impacts: Warnings about PNW's unacceptable environmental impacts

---

between resource-driven development and environmental regulation. To better understand the differences between the sample media in addressing these issues, I employed ADA and qualitatively interpreted relevant discursive representations in the dataset.

1.4. Structure of the Book

The rest of the book is organized as follows. Chapter 2 delves into the intricate relationships between fossil fuels, capitalism, and communication. The objective is to explicate the unique role energy transitions have played in capitalism's evolution, as well as the growing importance of communication in mediating energy–society relations. The chapter also reviews previous research on media coverage of extractivism, which serves as an important theoretical foundation for the empirical analysis of the BC LNG controversy. Chapter 3 continues the theoretical discussion by explicating the profound changes fracking has brought to global energy markets, scientific facts concerning this new extraction method's devastating environmental impacts, and previous research on related controversies in the United States and Europe. The chapter then provides a brief historical review of British Columbia's natural gas industry, with a focus on the industry's structural constraints as revealed by its previous failed attempts to connect with Asian markets.

The next three chapters present empirical findings with respect to public debates over BC LNG. These chapters follow a top-down analytical process, starting by making a set of arguments and then validating them by analyzing empirical evidence. Chapters 4 and 5 examine the pro- and anti-LNG storylines, respectively. The major findings regarding the discursive struggles between LNG proponents and opponents complicate the traditional "jobs versus the environment" dichotomy. The pro-LNG coalition made concerted efforts to articulate a progressive version of extractivism to legitimize LNG projects, while the anti-LNG coalition went beyond conventional environmental critiques and constructed a series of arguments attacking BC LNG's economic absurdity. Next, Chapter 6 assesses how Canadian media adopted both narratives by analyzing PNW news coverage. While public and commercial media were insensitive to the internal contradictions of transnational energy trade and used environmentalists and activists as scapegoats for the eventual cancellation of PNW, independent media made a significant contribution to broader public debates about the inherent economic risks of extreme carbon and the urgency of energy transition.

Chapter 7 concludes by summarizing the key findings of the preceding chapters and reflecting on Canada's current paradigm of progressive extractivism. Drawing on the research findings, I discuss the conditions required for a structural transformation of Canada's energy politics and the implications of the BC LNG case for future research on energy communication.

References

BC LNG: AltaGas Shelves Douglas Channel Project Near Kitimat. (2016, February 25). *CBC News*. www.cbc.ca

BC Ministry of Energy and Mines. (2012, February 03a). *Liquified natural gas: A strategy for British Columbia's newest industry*. https://vufind.llbc.leg.bc.ca/

BC Ministry of Natural Gas Development. (2013). *LNG 101: A guide to British Columbia's liquefied natural gas sector*. https://vufind.llbc.leg.bc.ca/

BC Office of the Premier. (2011, October 26). *Canada starts here: The BC jobs plan*. https://vufind.llbc.leg.bc.ca/

Bomberg, E. (2017). Shale we drill? Discourse dynamics in UK fracking debates. *Journal of Environmental Policy & Planning, 19*(1), 72–88. https://doi.org/10.1080/1523908X.2015.1053111

Chen, S., & Gunster, S. (2016). "Ethereal carbon": Legitimizing liquefied natural gas in British Columbia. *Environmental Communication, 10*(3), 305–321. https://doi.org/10.1080/17524032.2015.1133435

Chun, E. (2021). What Canada did – and didn't do – at the UN climate summit. *CBC News*. www.cbc.ca

Cox, R. (2007). Nature's "crisis disciplines": Does environmental communication have an ethical duty? *Environmental Communication, 1*(1), 5–20. https://doi.org/10.1080/17524030701333948

Davidson, D. J., & Gismondi, M. (2011). *Challenging legitimacy at the precipice of energy calamity*. Springer.

Dodge, J., & Lee, J. (2017). Framing dynamics and political gridlock: The curious case of hydraulic fracturing in New York. *Journal of Environmental Policy & Planning, 19*(1), 14–34. https://doi.org/10.1080/1523908X.2015.1116378

Dryzek, J. S. (2013). *The politics of the earth: Environmental discourses* (3rd ed.). Oxford University Press.

Eagle, R. (2017, March 23). Four decades and counting: A brief history of the Site C dam. *DeSmog Canada*. www.desmog.ca

Fast, T. (2014). Stapled to the front door: Neoliberal extractivism in Canada. *Studies in Political Economy, 94*(3), 31–60. https://doi.org/10.1080/19187033.2014.11574953

Fischer, F. (2003). *Reframing public policy: Discursive politics and deliberative practices*. Oxford University Press.

Garvie, K., Lowe, L., & Shaw, K. (2014). Shale gas development in Fort Nelson first nation territory: Potential regional impacts of the LNG boom. *BC Studies, 184*, 45–72.

Ghoussoub, M. (2017, July 25). Pacific NorthWest LNG project in Port Edward, BC, no longer proceeding. *CBC News*. www.cbc.ca

Gomes, I. (2015). *Natural gas in Canada: What are the options going forward?* Oxford Institute for Energy Studies. www.oxfordenergy.org/

Graham, N. (2017). State-capital nexus and the making of BC shale and liquefied natural gas. *BC Studies, 194*, 11–38.

Gunster, S. (2014). Storylines in the Sands: News, Narrative, and Ideology in the Calgary Herald. *Canadian Journal of Communication, 39*(3), 1–27. https://doi.org/10.22230/cjc.2014v39n3a2830

Gunster, S., Szeman, I., Greaves, M., & Neubauer, R. J. (2018). Communicating power: Energy, Canada, and the field(s) of communication. *Canadian Journal of Communication, 43*(1), 3–13.

Hackett, R. A., & Adams, P. R. (2018). *Jobs vs the environment? Mainstream and alternative media coverage of pipeline controversies*. Canadian Centre for Policy Alternatives. www.policyalternatives.ca

Hajer, M. A. (1995). *The politics of environmental discourse: Ecological modernization and the policy process*. Oxford University Press.

Hajer, M. A. (2005). Coalitions, practices, and meaning in environmental politics: From acid rain to BSE. In D. Howarth & J. Torfing (Eds.), *Discourse theory and European politics* (pp. 299–315). Palgrave Macmillan.

Hussain, Y. (2016, February 5). Shell delays B.C. LNG decision; 'Enormous uncertainty'. *The National Post*, p. FP1.

Jeong, J. (2019, January 8). The Wet'suwet'en and BC's gas-pipeline battle: A guide to the story so far. *The Globe and Mail*. www.theglobeandmail.com/

Lee, M. (2014). LNG: British Columbia's quest for a new staple industry. In J. Stanford (Ed.), *The staple theory @ 50* (pp. 80–83). Canadian Centre for Policy Alternatives.

Matthews J., & Hansen, A. (2018). Fracturing debate? A review of research on media coverage of "fracking". *Frontiers in Communication, 3*, item 41. https://doi.org/10.3389/fcomm.2018.00041

Metze, T. (2017). Fracking the debate: Frame shifts and boundary work in Dutch decision making on shale gas. *Journal of Environmental Policy & Planning, 19*(1), 3552, https://doi.org/10.1080/1523908X.2014.941462

Metze, T., & Dodge, J. (2016). Dynamic discourse coalitions on hydro-fracking in Europe and the United States. *Environmental Communication, 10*(3), 365–379, https://doi.org/10.1080/17524032.2015.1133437

Neubauer, R. (2018). Moving beyond the petrostate: Northern gateway, extractivism, and the Canadian petrobloc. *Studies in Political Economy, 99*(3), 246–267. https://doi.org/10.1080/07078552.2018.1536369

Olive, A., & Delshad, A. B. (2017). Fracking and framing: A comparative analysis of media coverage of hydraulic fracturing in Canadian and U.S. newspapers. *Environmental Communication, 11*(6), 784–799, https://doi.org/10.1080/17524032.2016.1275734

Owen, L. H. (2018, January 17). "We stepped in and started doing it": How one woman built an award-winning news outlet from her dining room table. *Nieman Lab*. https://www.niemanlab.org/

Petronas May Pull Out of BC LNG Project. (2014, September 25). *CBC News*. Retrieved May 18, 2018, from www.cbc.ca/news

Petronas to Spend up to $16B on BC LNG Project. (2013, June 11). *CBC News*. www.cbc.ca

Pineault, É. (2018). The capitalist pressure to extract: The ecological and political economy of extreme oil in Canada. *Studies in Political Economy, 99*(2), 130–150. https://doi.org/10.1080/07078552.2018.1492063

Rankin, E., & McElroy, J. (2017, April 11). Fact check: Promises, promises – last election's 'epic fail'. *CBC News*. www.cbc.ca

Tasker, J. P. (2016, September 27). Federal government approves liquefied natural gas project on BC coast with 190 conditions. *CBC News*. www.cbc.ca

Veltmeyer, H., & Bowles, P. (2014). Extractivist resistance: The case of the Enbridge oil pipeline project in Northern British Columbia. *The Extractive Industries and Society, 1*(1), 59–68.

Wilson, J. (1999). *Talk and log: Wilderness politics in British Columbia*. UBC Press.

Wylie, S. A. (2018). *Fractivism: Corporate bodies and chemical bonds*. Duke University Press.

2 Fossil Fuels, Capitalism, and Communication

Capitalism's ever-growing demand for fossil fuels has resulted in multiple environmental crises (e.g., air pollution, groundwater contamination, climate change, etc.) threatening the very survival of humanity (Forster & Clark, 2012 December 01; Klein, 2014; Intergovernmental Panel on Climate Change, 2022). As evidenced by increasingly sever and frequent extreme weather events, the pace of decarbonizing the global economy will profoundly shape humanity's future (Buck, 2021; Klein, 2014). This urgent situation has prompted a growing body of interdisciplinary scholarship, known as the energy humanities, which investigates the relationships between energy and society.

This chapter reviews the energy humanities' inquiries into the factors underpinning capitalism's insatiable demand for fossil fuels. Below, it begins with an overview of how the energy humanities approach the socio-political and ideological impacts of fossil fuels. This is followed by a discussion of the "staples trap" in Canada's political economy and its recent changes since the global primary commodities boom of the early 2000s. The next section reviews recent communication research on extractivism. The final section concludes the chapter by recognizing the discursive struggles over the development of liquefied natural gas (LNG) in British Columbia (BC) as illustrative of divergent public responses to the growing importance of unconventional fossil fuels in global capitalism. Taken together, the chapter explicates how the nexus between energy and capitalist social reproduction governs contemporary society. Globally escalating political conflicts over unconventional fossil fuels represent a growing backlash against energy-intensive forms of social production – the cornerstone of capitalist accumulation since the Industrial Revolution.

2.1. Capitalism and Energy Transition

Energy is essential for maintaining and enhancing the quality of human life. According to Smil (2017), there are three essential components of an energy system: "natural energy sources, their conversions, and specific uses of energy

DOI: 10.4324/9781003350620-2

flows" (p. 1). The systems of energy production, distribution, and consumption, by generating diverse and often highly unequal economic, political, and social patterns, structure the basic contours of a given historical period (Di Muzio, 2015; Urry, 2013). For example, the West's adoption of coal-based steam power during the 19th century granted it considerable energy surplus and set it onto a different developmental path from the East (Urry, 2014). Meanwhile, the omnipresence of oil during the 20th century laid the material foundation for modernization's vision of socio-political changes, notably mobility, urbanization, and globalization (Szeman, 2013; Wilson et al., 2017).

With climate change dramatically enhancing the visibility of fossil fuels, however, there has been growing public outcry for immediate actions to radically reduce Greenhouse Gas (GHG) emissions. This sense of urgency gives rise to the interdisciplinary field of energy humanities, which considers energy problems as challenges concerning ethics, beliefs, habits, institutions, and power. According to Wilson and her colleagues (2017), the field "positions oil and energy as the fulcrum around which many of today's most pressing social, economic, and political issues must be analysed and understood" (p. 4).

Following the tradition of ecocriticism, energy humanities scholarship conceptualizes energy as a vital factor in human history with both material and ideological impacts. These impacts tend to be hidden in social reproduction, but their significance has manifested in important periods of historical transition. For instance, by analyzing how the extraction and distribution of coal gave rise to modern forms of organized labor, Mitchell (2009) demonstrates the significant influence that labor resistance in coal mining had on the emergence of early democratic power under industrial capitalism. Likewise, Huber (2013) proposes that the pillars of "American life" – mobility, entrepreneurship, and suburban living – derive from the prevalence of private car ownership and the perception of oil as a cheap and seemingly inexhaustible energy source.

There are two areas of inquiry within the energy humanities that are vitally relevant for comprehending how fossil fuels impact resource-dependent economies like Canada. The first is the "petro-state" thesis and its related "staple resource bias" (Kennedy, 2014; Matthews, 2014). The second is "petro-culture" and its underlying anthropocentric values (Szeman, 2013; Wilson et al., 2017). The original petro-state thesis, first elaborated by Karl (1997), addresses the question of why oil-exporting states, notably developing economies in the Middle East, seemed unable to draw on their substantial oil revenues to build self-sustaining and stable developmental paths. Karl's explanation is that as many capital-deficient oil-exporting states employ the model of state ownership of oil resources, the state becomes the primary rent-seeking subject, which in turn produces institutional settings with blurred economic and political rationales.

Following the proliferation of petro-state research from economic geography to contingent fields, the term petro-state is now also used to describe the oil-driven economic development in countries such as Russia and Canada, wherein oil ought to be understood as a political resource enabling the energy sector to dominate public policymaking (Kennedy, 2014). Oil is an essential part of contemporary petro-states' territorial frameworks and it has embedded itself in everyday life in these states physically, legally, and culturally (Bridge & Le Billon, 2012). When applying the petro-state thesis to Canada, where the majority of energy corporations are privately owned, the primary focus of analysis is how state policies and actions have consistently prioritized the interests of the 'petro-bloc' – a constellation formed by institutions, social groups, and ideas dedicated to the expansion of bitumen production (Neubauer, 2018) – over those of other social segments.

If the petro-state thesis sheds light on the political transformations of the Canadian state over recent decades, then the concept of petro-culture attends to how fossil fuel dependency functions as an epistemological force structuring sociocultural imagination. Petro-culture research investigates how fossil fuels structure neoliberal "social reality" and contemporary social thoughts (Bridge & Le Billon, 2012; Huber, 2013; Wilson et al., 2017). According to Szeman (2013), there are three basic epistemological stances within contemporary oil politics and related public contestations: (1) strategic realism, which focusses primarily on how governments secure ongoing access to volatile supplies of petrocarbons, (2) techno-utopianism, which imagines technological solutions as the savior, maintaining and even improving the current economic and social status, and (3) eco-apocalypse, which recognizes the enormous risks of carbon dependency and insists on the need to fundamentally change contemporary societies. Petro-culture engages mainly with the first two: it defines oil as the foundation of social prosperity and defends both the feasibility and necessity of maintaining the carbon-intensive status quo.

Canada presents a unique case to examine the "resource dependency" mindset pervading everyday life and the ongoing public resistance to it on multiple fronts. This mentality has been a defining factor of the country's political economy. In his pioneering work on this topic, Innis (1956) discussed how Canada's reliance on exporting staples to Europe has powerfully shaped its economic, political, and social evolutions. The "dependency road" thesis by Smythe (1981) placed a similar emphasis on Canada's "consciousness industry's" central role in legitimizing its subordinate role to the United States.

More recently, the political contests over Alberta bitumen vividly illustrate the continuing centrality of extractivism in Canadian social organization, politics, and culture. Driven by a rapidly growing bitumen industry, Canada is well on its way to "dependency road 2.0", with its petro-bloc searching eagerly for new trading partners outside of North America (Matthews, 2014; Tindall, 2014). Compared with other prominent extractivist states (e.g., Russia and Venezuela), however, the Canadian petro-bloc relies heavily on covert ideological work to suppress public opposition to energy infrastructure projects, especially outside Alberta. Accordingly, this book's analysis of the public debates surrounding LNG development in British Columbia – Alberta's neighboring province – provides an intriguing case elucidating the inherent contradictions of Canadian fossil fuel discourses.

Considering that the BC LNG case is part of capitalism's systemic push for "extreme carbon" (i.e., unconventional fossil fuels trapped in geological formations with poor permeability and porosity), it is necessary to conduct a brief historical review of the rise of fossil fuels under capitalism, thereby reflecting on the energy–society relations during this historical process. According to the energy humanities, fossil fuels have shaped capitalism since its infancy and are the driving force behind the perpetual process of "accumulation by dispossession" – the basis of capitalism's exponential growth (Harvey, 2011). The transition to steam power marked not only the beginning of humanity's large-scale exploitation of highly concentrated stores of buried solar energy but also the birth of a fossil fuel economy – "an economy characterized by self-sustaining growth predicated on growing consumption of fossil fuels" (Malm, 2013, p. 17). Governing this economic mode is "petro-market civilization", which Di Muzio (2015) defines as "an historical and contradictory pattern of civilizational order whose social production is founded upon non-renewable fossil fuels, mediated by the price mechanism of the market and dominated by the logic of differential accumulation" (p. 5).

An understanding of the interconnection between fossil fuels and capitalist social reproduction must start with what gave rise to steam power. Conventional explanations for this question, known as the Ricardian-Malthusian paradigm (Wilkinson, 1973; Wrigley, 2010), can be summarized as follows: in the 18th century, Britain gradually ran out of streams suitable for running water mills, the dominant industrial power before steam. When the country's exponential economic growth demanded more industrial power, coal-based steam power stood out for its independence from water sources. The economic growth also led to a population explosion, which intensified the energy shortage and eventually forced the country to switch its energy base to coal. In short, the Ricardian-Malthusian paradigm emphasizes the interactions between the properties of different energy sources and socio-technical conditions, arguing that an energy transition moves beyond the niche phase more or less naturally when the advantages of an energy source become potent under certain social contexts. As for the case of steam engine versus water mill, the former won because of its wide availability.

The energy humanities, in contrast, examine the deeper connections between energy transition and the evolution of capitalism. For instance, Malm's (2013) analysis of the swift expansion of steam engines during the first half of the 19th century highlights two parallel processes brought by steam power's appearance in the British cotton industry: the emergence of the factory system and the increasing mechanization of the production flow within it. Steam engines outpaced water wheels – despite the latter being abundant, equally powerful, and generally cheaper – because the former created conditions for the stronger exploitation of labor. Back then, many streams were in remote areas which lacked skilled and disciplined labor, whereas steam engines could be used in populous towns or cities where large concentrations of workers enabled the possibility of lower wages due to competition for employment. Not constrained by the flow of water, capitalism became mobile, with "the freedom to seek out the populous towns, where labourers are easily procured" (Malm, 2013, p. 40). Despite being an expensive energy source throughout the 19th century, steam engines enabled capitalists to more effectively discipline and exploit the labor force. Steam engines thus replaced water wheels by offering more efficient exploitation of surplus value.

Whilst the growing coal sector in Northern Europe gave capitalists greater power over labor, it also enabled new forms of mass politics, which political theorist Timothy Mitchell (2009) defines as "carbon democracy". The energy networks transporting coal assembled large numbers of workers at their main junctions such as coal mines and railway stations. These junctions were so pivotal to capitalism that they became notable choke points within it, providing energy workers with a new kind of political power to make collective demands. Around the dawn of the 20th century, coal miners led labor activism and political mobilization across major industrial countries (Podobnik, 2006). If democracy is considered as striving for a more just world via collective actions, then coal miners' sabotage of capitalism's energy flow created political possibilities. In the words of Mitchell (2009), the political agency of energy workers "derived not just from the organizations they formed, the ideas they began to share or the political alliances they built, but from the extraordinary concentrations of carbon energy whose flow they could now slow, disrupt, or cut off" (p. 403).

The vulnerability experienced by capitalism forced it to look for means with which to constrain the political power of coal miners. In this context, oil presented an attractive alternative. The fluidity of oil makes it more energy-dense and transportable than coal, but these advantages were not the only factors that led to the swift development of oil production, which started first in the United States and Russia during the second half of the 19th century and then accelerated in the Middle East after World War II. A key factor driving North America and Europe to convert their primary energy source from coal to oil was the latter's ability to considerably lower the threat of working-class labor mobilization to carbon energy networks (Mitchell, 2009). Such reformulation of the capital–labor relationship was enabled by the notable differences between oil and coal in terms of production, distribution, and consumption. Firstly, oil requires a smaller workforce than coal because it is brought to the ground either by water or natural gas. Secondly, workers in the oil industry are under constant direct supervision by managers, as opposed to the relative autonomy of coal workers when they work underground. Thirdly, although pump stations and pipelines are still vulnerable to strike actions, incapacitating these energy infrastructures is not as easy as with railways. Fourthly, oil combustion produces much less residue than coal burning, which eliminated the need for stokers in the oil sector. Lastly but most importantly, the fluidity and relative lightness of oil allow it to be shipped across oceans in vast quantities. Taken together, these differences undermined the labor force's power to negotiate social contracts with capitalists. Consequently, labor unions in the fossil fuel industry worldwide achieved far less success than their coal-sector predecessors.

During the post-WWII era (1948–1973), the Keynesian-Fordist system further strengthened the centrality of oil to capitalism, which led to the increased refinement of petro-market civilization. The unprecedented recovery and expansion of capitalism during this era hinged on abundant, accessible, and affordable oil. As energy humanities scholars have argued (e.g., Huber, 2013; Mitchell, 2009; Urry, 2013), oil contributed to the new conception of unlimited economic growth in two ways. First, oil prices remained exceptionally low between 1948 and 1973. Second, oil was treated as an inexhaustible resource because of the Middle East's expanding capacities in oil production and transportation. The central role of oil in the post-WWII global economy was well reflected in the postwar global financial order, which was built on oil flows instead of gold reserves. Although the Bretton Woods system defined the US dollar as the global currency by pegging its value to gold, in practice, the value of US currency was maintained by its convertibility to oil since "in both value and volume, oil was the largest commodity in world trade" (Mitchell, 2009, p. 414).

The postwar economic boom also stimulated private car ownership, which gradually provided the ideological foundation of the "American way of life". In North America, driving is often considered not a free choice but a necessity. The prevalence of car-based living allows the mass dispersal of the urban population throughout a sprawling metropolis, with suburban communities being built far from city centers (Huber, 2013). Associated with the process of suburbanization is a less cohesive, fragmentary social structure symbolized by single-family houses. To a large extent, such houses naturalize high energy consumption since they are equipped with household goods (e.g., television, refrigerator, and oven) whose manufacture and usage are energy intensive. Further needs in suburbs are often met by town centers where chain stores, supermarkets, and leisure sites operate. The maintenance of these facilities involves the long-distance movement of many commodities, which requires the burning of oil. In sum, the process of suburbanization consists of energized practices that actively shape the public's perceptions and feelings about life, politics, and culture.

Driving constantly mediates the fragmentary nature of suburban life by acting as a solution to everyday challenges. Overcoming these challenges offers deeply felt visions of satisfaction, freedom, and individualism, which makes the public increasingly view both physical and social spaces as vast, open territories to be conquered by individual choices. Private car ownership expands machinery into everyday life and helps to subsume life into capitalism. By fuelling the unprecedented expansion of individualized mobility, oil has constructed the "American way of life" around automobility, single-family housing, and privatized social production. Ideologically, this lifestyle encourages an entrepreneurial attitude, key to which is the idea that "life is structured by a social field wherein wealth and material goods justifiably flow into privatized hands that work hard to achieve a particular material standard of life" (Huber, 2013 p. xiv).

From this perspective, the rise of neoliberalism was closely related to the petro-based "American way of life", which celebrates the ideological triumph of petro-market civilization. Radical political economy (e.g., Harvey, 2007; McNally, 2011) tends to claim that neoliberalism, as an economic–political–ideological complex, gained popularity following the collapse of the Keynesian-Fordist system during the 1970s. However, considering how the rise of neo-conservatism and the privatization of social space went hand in hand, then oil's saturation of suburban life and the populist hatred of government interventions mobilized the rise of the neoliberal hegemony. Accordingly, the postwar period (1948–1973) must be viewed as neoliberalism's incubation period wherein a popular resentment of government, taxes, and Keynesianism accumulated. This resentment eventually erupted when the political moment of opportunity emerged in the 1970s.

Despite sustaining a quarter-century-long postwar boom in major capitalist countries, the Keynesian-Fordist system was hit by a series of structural crises during the 1970s. McNally (2011) deems the 1971–1982 economic stagnation as a "global slump" period characterized by reduced economic activity, job loss, and an inflationary wave. In his view, declining profitability caused by over-accumulation was ultimately responsible for the recession. It should be noted that the global slump period was accompanied by fundamental changes in the global energy landscape. Preceding the decade-long recession was the 1967–1974 oil crisis, which dismantled the Bretton Woods system (Mitchell, 2009). This crisis coincided with notable power shifts in transatlantic oil trade. The dominant role of Gulf states in the Organization for Petroleum Exporting Countries (OPEC) was decisive in the launch of the 1973–1974 oil embargo, and the significant impacts of this action revealed the potential of oil as a political weapon.

Rising environmental concerns also drove the global energy landscape's restructuring process (Mitchell, 2009; Urry, 2013). Influential publications such as *Silent Spring* (Carson 1962), *The Limits to Growth* (Meadows et al., 1972), and *Small Is Beautiful* (Schumacher, 1973) successfully drew public attention to the adverse impacts of unbridled economic growth. In collaboration with anti-war and civil rights activists, environmentalists developed the image of the "vulnerable Earth" and framed the environment as a new object of politics for which the fossil fuel industry must be held responsible. The first Earth Day was celebrated in 1970.

Thus, if the Keynesian-Fordist system was sustained by abundant, accessible, and affordable oil, it became clear in the early 1980s that the system had been sabotaged by the persistent threat of "peak oil" (Di Muzio, 2015). Although capitalism managed to restore profitability through neoliberalism and its associated "flexible accumulation" regime – as marked by a series of reconfigurations in labor relationships, the role of the government, and the global organization of production (Harvey, 2007; McNally, 2011), it was unable to address the contradiction of a pro-market civilization built ultimately on non-renewable hydrocarbon reserves.

Global energy demand continued to grow rapidly after neoliberalism eventually brought the rest of the world into market relations during the 1990s. Today, as Urry (2013) points out, we have entered a peak moment of petro-market civilization. The paradox lies in the fact that many countries are still in the process of achieving modernization and prosperity at a time when climate change reveals the environmentally destructive nature of petro-market civilization. Meanwhile, given the increasing difficulty and cost of conventional oil and gas extraction, capitalist social reproduction is subject to an imminent, permanent decline in energy supply.

It is this circumstance that prompts global capitalism to aggressively pursue the exploitation of unconventional fossil fuels (i.e., "extreme carbon") via new extraction technologies such as fracking and offshore drilling. British Columbia's ambition of developing a LNG sector targeting Asian markets can be viewed as a direct outcome of this trend. The access to previously inaccessible deposits has drastically altered the global energy landscape and amplified the social visibility of extractivism. The era of extreme carbon effectively sustains the world's dependence on accessible, cheap, and abundant energy. The harsh climate reality, however, requires that most extreme carbon be left underground (Coffin & Grant, 2019). In this context, energy humanities scholars have become increasingly interested in the complex interplays between energy and political power (Wilson et al., 2017).

2.2. Extractivism and the "Staples Trap" in Canadian Policymaking

Booming global extreme carbon production exposes the developmental, societal, political, and ecological contradictions of extractivism, which is defined in the development studies literature as a capital accumulation model predicated primarily on the extraction and export of natural resources (Acosta, 2013; Brand et al., 2016; Burchardt & Dietz, 2014). Extractivism demonstrates "accumulation by dispossession" (Harvey, 2011), the process by which capitalism relentlessly advances predatory practices targeting "non-productive" lands and natural resources. Facilitating these practices are neoliberal policies, such as privatization, deregulation, and trans-nationalization.

Extractivism is also "a mechanism of colonial and neo-colonial plunder and appropriation" (Acosta, 2013, p. 63). It sustains the industrial development and prosperity of capitalism's metropolitan centres by trapping certain countries and regions in the "resource curse". In such countries and regions, transnational corporations often dominate the exploitation of natural resources and the appropriation of profits whereas governments maintain the momentum of resource-dependent development through economic, political, and ideological structures (Burchardt & Dietz, 2014).

The national development strategies of several left-leaning governments in Latin America (e.g., Bolivia, Ecuador, and Venezuela) since the early 2000s have prompted scholarly discussions on whether the region's developmental path has embraced "neo-extractivism", which partially breaks with neoliberalism. Compared with conventional extractivism, which is typically justified by corporate social responsibility or market fundamentalism, neo-extractivism acquires its legitimacy through national–populist and anti-colonial sentiments. Venezuela under Hugo Chávez, for instance, explicitly stated that its oil and gas industry was of the people and for the people. Representative neo-extractivist policies legitimize the exploitation of nature by emphasizing its indispensable contributions to national development, sovereignty, and social redistribution (Brand et al., 2016; Burchardt & Dietz, 2014; Svampa, 2015). Such policies include the nationalization of key resource sectors, stronger government oversight of resource extraction and the improved use of surplus revenue to enhance the material well-being of ordinary citizens.

With respect to social and ecological contradictions, however, neo-extractivism still shares many similarities with conventional extractivism. Although neo-extractivism seeks to resist neoliberalism's adverse impacts on Latin America, it still relies on developed capitalist countries' perpetual demand for primary commodities. Additionally, left-leaning government oversight does not alter the anthropocentric nature of resource extraction, which reconfigures spatial, social, and labor relations by driving the enclosure and commodification of the natural commons (Burchardt & Dietz, 2014). Threatened by these contradictions, various forms of citizen resistance, in conjunction with strengthening Indigenous movements, mobilize more and more concerned citizens to defend the commons, biodiversity, and the environment (Svampa, 2015).

Mirroring the changes in Latin America's resource sector, Canada has witnessed significant growth in exports of raw and near-raw materials, a gradual decline of the manufacturing sector, and a continuous wave of foreign direct-investment inflows since the early 2000s (Fast, 2014). These economic trends have ramped up scholarly and public concern regarding the revival of the "staples trap" in Canadian policymaking, which exhibits both similarities and differences to Latin America's neo-extractivism. Similar to Latin America,

Canada's resource-driven development trajectory has produced an "export mentality" (Gunton, 2014), which serves as a double-edged sword for domestic economic development: while it brings wealth to Canada and generates high returns on investment, it also places the country in a structurally vulnerable position in the global economy.

Compared with Latin America, Canada plays a dual role in global extractive chains. On the one hand, Canadian capital is becoming increasingly outwardly oriented: many Canadian corporations play leading roles in driving natural resource industries in the global South. On the other hand, transnational ownership has a strong presence in the Canadian oil and gas sector. In British Columbia, for instance, transnational energy corporations such as Kinder Morgan, Petronas, and Sinopec have been important yet barely visible stakeholders behind political contests concerning energy infrastructure.

Research on the staples trap was first popularized by Harold Innis (1956), whose analysis of Canadian economic history elucidated how staples made the country primarily a hinterland for other industrial economies in the first half of the 20th century. During this period, Canada's domestic innovation, manufacturing, and technological capacity gave way to the development of resource extraction and transportation infrastructure. These structural imbalances exposed the domestic economy and resource-dependent communities in particular to the volatile boom-and-bust cycles of global capitalism. At the heart of Innis' insights into Canadian economic history is the distinction between central and peripheral sites within the global capitalist system (Cameron, 2014; MacNeil, 2014; Watkins, 2007). Whilst the former drive capitalist production and innovation, the latter are reduced to serving as resource bases.

Many political economists have studied Canada's dependency on staples following Innis. The most notable among them is Mel Watkins, who in his seminal essay "A Staple Theory of Economic Growth" (1963) advanced Innis's historical insights by identifying three industrial linkages within the production of staples: the "backward linkage" for the staple-producing machinery, the "forward linkage" for the staple-processing machinery, and the "final demand linkage" for staple consumption. Watkins argued that one way to escape the staples trap is through public and private investments that strengthen industrial links. For example, the formation of Canada's industrial base (especially in Ontario and Quebec) during the post-WWII era resulted from the outcome of effective tariff policies, which kept domestic businesses from being swamped by the adjacent US economy. By facilitating domestic job creation, the tariff wall also stimulated the expansion of demand for consumer goods and associated industries. Accordingly, state interventions against laissez-faire capitalism played a pivotal role in breaking the pattern of resource-led development.

According to Watkins, Canada's experience with the staples trap results in both an economic development model and a policymaking mindset. In accordance with this view, Dallas Smythe (1981) discussed how the history of

Canada's communication sector followed a "dependency road" resembling the country's staple dependency. As the country's telecommunication, television, radio, cinema, and book publishing grew and became increasingly dependent on US enterprises, they collectively served as a "consciousness industry", distributing US cultural products to the Canadian public and immersing them in American consumer values and habits.

The critical approach to the staples trap, as developed by Innis, Watkins, Smythe, and many other political economists, remains a productive field within critical social sciences in Canada today, especially with respect to the economic, political, and cultural dynamics surrounding the fossil fuel industry. In the context of a primary commodities boom led by global economic shifts (notably the rise of new industrial countries like China and India), Canada has returned to its historical pattern of staple-driven economic growth in recent years (Cameron, 2014: Fast, 2014; Veltmeyer & Bowles, 2014; Watkins, 2007).

The bitumen industry in Alberta, currently Canada's largest staple-based economic expansion, is emblematic of how extractivism reshapes local and national economies (Davidson & Gismondi, 2011; Pineault, 2018). Located primarily in three deposits (Athabasca, Cold Lake, and Peace River), Alberta's reserves of bitumen are estimated at 1.7 to 2.5 trillion barrels of crude oil, making the province the largest single deposit of crude in the world (Clark et al., 2013). Although the commercial extraction of bitumen was initiated back in the early 1960s, it was until the 2000s that the industry began to experience unprecedented growth.

Two major factors initiated this boom. First, high oil prices during the 2000s made the bitumen industry extremely profitable, which led to the Canadian Energy Research Institute's (Honarvar et al., 2011) optimistic prediction that the growth of the bitumen sector between 2010 and 2035 would generate 830,000 new jobs, $2.1 trillion GDP, and $311 billion in tax revenue for Canada (including $105 billion for Alberta). Second, Canadian bitumen presents a viable avenue by which countries like the United States and China can meet their energy needs and reduce their reliance on Middle Eastern sources. In recent years, bitumen has overshadowed forestry, agriculture, and fishery as the primary contributor to Canada's trade account, becoming a "super staple" deeply ingrained in national capitalism and society (Gunton, 2014).

The bitumen industry's expansion exhibits several typical characteristics of a staple-led development. The acceleration of this expansion derives from spikes in global oil prices, over which Canada has little control. Pipelines aimed at enhancing bitumen's access to "tidewater" – notably the Northern Gateway pipeline project, the Energy East pipeline project, the Keystone XL project, and the Trans Mountain pipeline expansion – were all proposed and planned based on the optimistic assumption that the global price for crude oil would stay above $100 per barrel (Neubauer, 2018). Nonetheless, the unpredictability of global demand and supply resulted in substantial price volatility during the 2010s, vividly illustrating the risk posed by the boom-and-bust cycle to mega energy projects.

Many bitumen producers in Alberta are controlled by transnational energy conglomerates that rely on foreign-located forwards and backwards linkages rather than developing domestic infrastructure. The majority of bitumen extracted in Canada is exported unprocessed to foreign refineries. The industry argues that raw bitumen is not upgraded into crude in Alberta because it is not capital efficient to build refineries there when such facilities already exist in other places, but such an argument also reinforces the profitability of foreign ownership. Ideally, maximizing the economic benefit of a staple requires distributing the collected rent (relatively) equally amongst the owners of the staple (Watkins, 2007), but in the case of bitumen, available evidence indicates that not only is the revenue retained in one region (i.e., Alberta), but extractive capital also exploits a large proportion of it (Clark et al, 2013; Davidson & Gismondi, 2011).

As Canada becomes increasingly dependent on bitumen and other resource sectors to earn foreign exchange, its economy has demonstrated symptoms of the "Dutch disease". The term was coined in a 1977 article in the *Economist* that discussed the economic implications on the Dutch economy of the discovery of the Groningen gas field in the 1960s. The vast amounts of foreign capital drawn into the Netherlands significantly inflated its national currency, and, consequently, Dutch manufactures were priced out of domestic and international markets.

A similar process has occurred in the context of Alberta bitumen. Prior to the 2014 global oil price collapse, the rising exchange rates of the Canadian dollar had considerably undermined the competitiveness of Canadian manufacturing. In 2012, the then-leader of the federal New Democratic Party (NDP), Thomas Mulcair, attributed the loss of manufacturing jobs in Canada to a Dutch disease associated with the bitumen boom. This remark sparked a public controversy, making "Dutch disease" an ideologically charged term in Canadian public discourse (Gollom, 2012 May 18). In hindsight, Mulcair's remark was "poor politics, but sound economics" (Fitz-Morris, 2015 April 14): the hollowing out of Canadian manufacturing was confirmed by a 2014 Bank of Canada analysis, which found that "the sector has lost 75% of its output since 2000" (para. 10).

Ideologically, the bitumen boom has fostered a "dependency mindset" extolling resource extraction and export in economic policymaking. Representative articulations of this mindset include the "Canada as an energy superpower" narrative from former Prime Minister Stephen Harper (Clark et al., 2013), the public outreach campaign "Canada's Energy Citizens" (Wood, 2018) by the Canadian Association of Petroleum Producers (CAPP), and the promotion of pipeline projects as a "nation-building" mechanism by CAPP and other fossil fuel proponents (Barney, 2017). These pro-bitumen discourses collectively legitimize the further expansion of extractivism by celebrating oil's ubiquity in modern life and referring to it as part of Canada's national identity. As exemplified by the Northern Gateway Pipeline controversy, the emerging petro-public in the Canadian public sphere, backed by industry-supporting political and economic elites, has significant potential to redefine Canadian nationalism in relation to the country's status as a petro-state (Neubauer, 2018).

Besides strengthening the staples model of development, the bitumen boom has also led to devastating social and environmental impacts. As an unconventional petroleum deposit, bitumen exists in a natural mixture of sand, clay, and rock. During a typical bitumen mining process, this synthetic crude is surface-mined, and crude oil is extracted through an energy-intensive process using either water or steam. The extraction and refinement process of bitumen entails much higher environmental costs than conventional crude oil, such as air pollution, groundwater contamination, the destruction of wildlife habitats and virgin boreal forest, high energy consumption (during bitumen production), and significant GHG emissions (Nikiforuk, 2010).

As for social impacts, communities adjacent to bitumen infrastructure are confronted with mounting social problems such as public health issues, housing shortages, substance abuse, and food insecurity. Many of such communities are occupied by First Nations, whose traditions and Indigenous rights are also under direct threat. Although Canada's current regulatory regime requires the bitumen industry to engage in meaningful consultation and seek accommodation of Indigenous interests in resource development, Impact and Benefit Agreements (IBAs) – the primary mechanism via which First Nations negotiate with corporations – are "functioning as tools for the privatization of the federal duty to consult Indigenous peoples about resource development on their lands, naturalizing market-based solutions to social suffering, and limiting access to important political and legal channels" (Cameron & Levitan, 2014). Perhaps more disturbing is the politics of dispossession characterizing the bitumen expansion. With the appropriation of Indigenous lands and the exploitation of both settler and Indigenous labour forces, the bitumen sector reinforces Canadian settler colonialism with policies and legislations which "revolve around land theft and Indigenous erasure to facilitate the permanent settlement of non-Indigenous exalted subjects" (Preston, 2017, p. 354).

Overall, the bitumen boom occurs in the context of an ongoing global restructuring of capitalism. Besides its established trade partnerships with the United States and European countries, Canada now actively seeks to sell its natural resources to emerging industrial powers such as China and India. The local, national, and international resistance against bitumen reveals the negative consequences brought by this super staple to Canada's economic, social, and environmental sustainability. As Pineault (2016 May 18) argues, the bitumen boom has initiated the age of "extreme oil", a time of struggle between the imperatives of decarbonizing the global economy and protecting the asset value of unconventional fossil fuel reserves.

2.3. Communication Research on Extreme Carbon

Despite the aforementioned high social and environmental costs, the economic and political appeals of bitumen continue to inspire many provincial governments in Canada. Since the early 2000s, there have been numerous proposals across Canada to increase the extraction and export of fossil fuels, with BC LNG's ambitious scale making it the most notable "follower". The blueprint for LNG development in British Columbia borrows numerous strategies from Alberta's bitumen policies and fits the classic pattern of resource-driven development: "seek foreign investment to tap our resources for export markets, secure jobs and income for Canadian workers, and use royalty and corporate tax revenue to help pay for public services, in lieu of personal taxation" (Lee, 2014, p. 81).

However, three notable shifts in Canada's energy politics since the 2010s have brought additional barriers against the aggressive promotion of extractive industries like BC LNG. First, the Canadian energy sector's economic performance over the decade of the 2010s – when North American oil and gas prices fluctuated around low levels – was disappointing to investors and the public. Second, Canada is bound by the carbon reduction goal of the Paris Agreement, which places increasing regulatory pressure on the oil and gas industry. Third, the growing political pressures of decolonization strengthen public opposition to the appropriation of Indigenous lands by Canadian extractivist industries.

In this context, public opposition to extractivism has gained momentum in the Canadian public sphere, raising important theoretical questions about energy communication. As a subfield of environmental communication, energy communication research consists of three noteworthy themes: "(1) the role of media in covering energy crises; (2) analyses of corporate communication surrounding crises; and (3) discourses of decision-making about energy in the context of crises" (Endres et al., 2016, p. 424). Informed by previous research on these themes, the empirical analysis presented in subsequent chapters will consider the BC LNG controversy as a discursive contestation in which various stakeholders seek to influence public opinion by constructing competing narratives on extreme carbon.

Extreme carbon, whether it be bitumen, shale gas, or other forms of unconventional fossil fuels, is a contentious policy issue in many countries (Bomberg, 2017; Dodge & Metze, 2017; Metze, 2017; Olive & Delshad, 2017). Conflicting interpretations of its economic and environmental implications co-exist in the public sphere as its proponents and opponents deploy various mobilizing frames to legitimize their opinions. Media coverage, for instance, portrays the expanding extreme carbon sector as a new revenue resource that will bring economic benefits and employment, a temporary solution that will provide energy security and facilitate the transition to a carbon-free society, or an environmental threat with significant impacts on the local environment and climate change.

Polarizing public perceptions and diverse government viewpoints of extreme carbon underscore the importance of researching the relationship between media and extractivism. In Canada, relevant studies have focused on how advertisements, newspapers, and social media, among others, communicate about the controversies surrounding energy infrastructure, particularly projects associated with the production and transportation of bitumen. Collectively, these studies demonstrate that the intensifying public disputes over Alberta bitumen reflect "an emerging, international flashpoint in the rising tension between economic development on the current, global model and its ecological costs" (Takach, 2013, p. 212).

For example, Friedel's (2008) analysis of bitumen advertising revealed how First Nations' bodies and landscapes are used as semiotic tropes to promote the neoliberal agendas of transnational energy conglomerates. Likewise, studies such as Remillard (2011) and Takach (2013) found that visual representations of bitumen, depending on how they address the tension between nature as sublime and nature as resource, could mobilize contradictory public perceptions of resource management and environmental degradation. The visual narratives on bitumen by Alberta government and energy corporations tend to reproduce extractivism's anthropocentric stance on nature. In terms of news coverage, there is an uptick in research examining how news influences public opinion about bitumen infrastructure. Kojola (2017), for instance, explored the representations of labor and the environment in media coverage of the Keystone XL Pipeline. His framing analysis revealed a persistent "jobs versus the environment" dichotomy dividing bitumen proponents and opponents. Papineau and Deacon (2017) found a similar pattern in local and national coverage of Fort McMurray, the city at the center of the bitumen boom.

Canadian energy communication research has also addressed the relationship between media agenda and policymaking. Drawing on a diversity of approaches to media effects, studies such as Gunster and Saurette (2014), Neubauer (2018), Raso and Neubauer (2016), and Way (2011) have explicated how bitumen advocates – notably politicians, energy corporations, pro-industry think tanks, and conservative ideologues – orchestrate pro-bitumen narratives. These narratives employ political and ideological manipulations to suppress public imaginations about alternative energy futures by effectively framing the "addiction to oil" as a "common sense of daily life" (Huber, 2013). For example, by framing anti-bitumen efforts as propaganda from foreign-funded radicals (Gunster & Saurette, 2014), the Alberta government incite the conflict between workers and environmentalists, thereby silencing alternatives. Similarly, research on media coverage of the Northern Gateway Pipeline (Dusyk et al., 2018; Neubauer, 2018) explicated how media's framing of the project as a trade-off between economic benefits and environment risks led to heightened public concerns over local impacts and regional distribution of risks and benefits, which subsequently paralyzed the inter-provincial negotiation process.

Besides studies explicating the role of media in public opinion and policy-making outcomes, communication scholarship on bitumen also takes a normative stance criticizing structural biases in the Canadian media system that favors extractivist voices. This media environment sets up a disproportionately structured discursive space that neglects the voices of scientists, environmental groups, and concerned citizens. Instead, it amplifies fossil fuel advocates who have framed bitumen as ethical and necessary for the Canadian economy (e.g., Levant, 2010). Conservative newspapers like the *National Post* and the *Calgary Herald* are deeply involved in building a convincing storyline depicting the bitumen industry as a victim under constant and aggressive attacks from environmental groups, which effectively undermines environmental critiques of the industry (Gunster & Saurette, 2014). Industry proponents and conservative think tanks facilitate this storyline by functioning as the primary voices in media texts, relegating bitumen oppositions to secondary positions (Raso & Neubauer, 2016).

The research on the conventional media's advocacy for extractivism in Canada reveals crucial structural aspects of the country's media system. Despite the increasing prevalence of independent media promoting participatory and solution-oriented journalism, traditional mass media and their online extensions remain one of the most influential storytellers in modern society. Conventional media content remains more authoritative and reliable than social media posts as references for policymakers (Callison & Tindall, 2017; Newman, 2011). Moreover, despite the fact that opinion pieces are typically less constrained by journalistic norms, they play an important role in discursive struggles between political camps because they provide interpretive frames for public debates.

One trend across the Canadian media system since the 2000s has been an increasingly concentrated media ownership in the news sector (Beaty, 2011; Winseck, 2019), which is of particular relevance to the current study as it further reinforces Canadian mass media's crucial role in setting the public agenda on energy issues. As summarized in the 2019 report from the Canadian Media Concentration Research Project (Winseck, 2019), the level of concentration across Canada's network media economy has risen significantly since 2000 as a result of several media acquisitions which dramatically increased the consolidation and vertical integration of Canadian media. Along with the concentration process and the decline of serious journalism, conventional media have become more vulnerable to corporate interests, which forms the basis of their editorial leaning towards the fossil fuel industry.

Take Postmedia Network as an example. A recent review (Edge, 2016) of this Canadian media conglomerate noted that "it now publishes 37.6% of Canadian paid daily newspaper circulation and owns fifteen of the twenty-two largest English language dailies, including 75.4% in the three westernmost provinces, where Postmedia owns eight of the nine largest dailies" (p. 53). Given that the political contests over bitumen and shale gas mainly concern the provinces of British Columbia and Alberta, the 75.4% figure is particularly concerning. Postmedia is an ideological ally and friendly voice of the fossil fuel industry. As described in a leaked presentation given to the Canadian Association of Petroleum Producers (CAPP), Postmedia has stated it is eager to "work with the Canadian oil and gas industry to bring energy to the forefront of our national conversation and engage executives, the business community and the Canadian public to underscore the ways in which the energy sector powers Canada" (cited in Gunster & Saurette, 2014, p. 335). Moreover, Postmedia is not alone in offering uncritical coverage of oil and gas.

In contrast, despite relatively high media visibility, the political efficacy of environmental organizations in Canada remain quite limited. In their comprehensive analysis of mediated policy networks within Canadian national news, Stoddart and his colleagues (2017) have attributed such lack of political efficacy to the concerted efforts by the petro-bloc, notably politicians and think tanks who circulated claims concerning bitumen's economic significance on behalf of the fossil fuel industry. Likewise, in a 2018 commentary published by the environmental news website *Narwhal*, activist David Gray-Donald (2018 August 13) has examined how major Canadian media reported on CAPP's 2018 Oil Outlook and found that, amongst the three news sources covering it, none pointed to the fact that CAPP's projections overtly broke the climate limits set in the Paris Agreement.

Given the conventional media's dwindling resources and refusal to report critically on the fossil fuel industry, activists use alternative methods to reach the general public. In British Columbia, fast-growing independent media have actively confronted concentrated media ownership since the early 2000s. By amplifying progressive perspectives on issues like sustainability, democracy, and Indigenous justice, these emerging public voices have created a "alternative public sphere" (Chen & Gunster, 2018). In their critical analysis of journalism and the climate crisis, Hackett and his colleagues (2017) argued that hegemonic media's focus on disaster, threat, and elite political squabbling creates a "hope gap" that leaves audiences, even those most alarmed by climate change, with a sense of disengagement and powerlessness, rather than efficacy. (p. 3). Thus, another objective of researching energy discourses is to demonstrate the capacity of independent media to close this "hope gap".

Echoing the insightful observation of Hackett and his colleagues (2017), the empirical analysis in subsequent chapters underscores the idea that fossil fuel discourses, advanced by governments and corporations via mass media, are a key contributor to the public legitimation of extreme carbon. By boosting doubt, fear, and even cynicism about a future global economy beyond fossil fuels, these discourses depict extreme carbon like bitumen and shale gas as the only viable choice for humanity. To develop "effective and empowering environmental communication" (Hackett et al., 2017), it is necessary to confront the legitimacy of extreme carbon with innovative discursive strategies, which this dissertation hypothesizes finding in LNG opponents' discourses.

2.4. Chapter Conclusion

This chapter elaborates the linkages between capitalism, fossil fuels, and communication to arrive at an analytical framework for examining the discursive struggles over LNG development in British Columbia. As explicated by energy humanities research on the historical evolution of capitalism, the climate crisis is an inevitable consequence of the dependence of capitalist accumulation on energy-intensive forms of social production. Decarbonizing the global economy thus necessitates knocking down the material and ideological pillars that legitimize fossil fuels as indispensable to socioeconomic prosperity. As Forster and Clark (2012 December 1) note,

> we have a generation at most in which to carry out a radical transformation in our economic relations, and our relations with the earth, if we want to avoid a major tipping point or "point of no return," after which vast changes in the earth's climate will likely be beyond our ability to prevent and will be irreversible.
>
> (para. 3)

However, industry analysts and policymakers continue to be captivated by the near-term economic potential of unconventional fossil fuels notwithstanding the urgency of reaching net-zero emissions. Although rapidly expanding unconventional fossil fuel production has mitigated the threat of a global energy shortage to capitalism's continued growth, the dominance of fossil fuels in the global energy landscape is no longer sustainable due to their rising economic, technical, and environmental costs (Urry, 2013). In this context, cases like BC LNG become controversies that reveal agonistic visions of the future of the global energy landscape.

Building on the previous theoretical insights, the next chapter will discuss how Canadian corporations and policymakers view unconventional fossil fuels as the nation's engine of economic growth in the 21st century. Situating Canada as a frontier of neoliberal extractivist development, it demonstrates how the BC Liberal government's ambition for LNG development was inspired by former Canadian Prime Minister Stephen Harper's "energy superpower" narrative and the huge success of Alberta's bitumen sector.

References

Acosta, A. (2013). Extractivism and neo-extractivism: Two sides of the same curse. In M. Lang & D. Mokrani (Eds.), *Beyond development: Alternative visions for Latin America* (pp. 61–86). Transnational Institute.

Barney, D. (2017). Who we are and what we do: Canada as a pipeline nation. In S. Wilson, A. Carlson, & I. Szeman (eds.), *Petrocultures: Oil, politics, culture* (pp. 78–119). McGill-Queen's University Press.

Beaty, B. (2011). Canada: Media system. In W. Donsbach, J. Byrant, & R. T. Craig (Eds.), *The international encyclopedia of communication* (online ed.). https://onlinelibrary.wiley.com/doi/10.1002/9781405186407.wbiecc002.pub2

Bomberg, E. (2017). Shale we drill? Discourse dynamics in UK fracking debates. *Journal of Environmental Policy & Planning, 19*(1), 72–88. https://doi.org/10.1080/1523908X.2015.1053111

Brand, U., Dietz, K., & Lang, M. (2016). Neo-Extractivism in Latin America: One side of a new phase of global capitalist dynamics. *Ciencia Política, 11*(21), 125–159. https://doi.org/10.15446/cp.v11n21.57551

Bridge, G., & Le Billon, P. (2012). *Oil*. Polity Press.

Buck, H. J. (2021). *Ending fossil fuels: Why net zero is not enough*. Verso.

Burchardt, H., & Dietz, K. (2014) (Neo-)extractivism – a new challenge for development theory from Latin America. *Third World Quarterly, 35*(3), 468–486. https://doi.org/10.1080/01436597.2014.893488

Callison, C., & Tindall, D. B. (2017). Climate change communication in Canada. In M. C. Nisbet, S. S. Ho, E. Markowitz, S. O'Neill, M. S. Schäfer, & J. Thaker (Eds.), *The Oxford encyclopedia of climate change communication* (online ed.). http://climatescience.oxfordre.com/view/10.1093/acrefore/9780190228620.001.0001/acrefore-9780190228620-e-477

Cameron, D. (2014). Watkins, Innis, and Canadian economics. In J. Stanford (Ed.), *The staple theory @ 50* (pp. 25–28). Canadian Centre for Policy Alternatives.

Cameron, E., & Levitan, T. (2014). Impact and benefit agreements and the neoliberalization of resource governance and Indigenous-state relations in Northern Canada. *Studies in Political Economy, 93*(1). 25–52. https://doi.org/10.1080/19187033.2014.11674963

Carson, R. (1962). *Silent spring*. Houghton Mifflin.

Chen, S., & Gunster, S. (2019) China as Janus: The framing of China by British Columbia's alternative public sphere. *Chinese Journal of Communication, 12*(4), 431–448. https://doi.org/10.1080/17544750.2018.1530686

Clark, T., Gibson, D., Haley, B., & Stanford, J. (2013). *The bitumen cliff: Lessons and challenges of bitumen mega-developments for Canada's economy in an age of climate change*. Canadian Centre for Policy Alternatives.

Coffin, M., & Grant, A. (2019). *Balancing the budget: Why deflating the carbon bubble requires oil and gas companies to shrink*. The Carbon Tracker Initiative. www.carbontracker.org/

Davidson, D. J., & Gismondi, M. (2011). *Challenging legitimacy at the precipice of energy calamity*. Springer.

Di Muzio, T. (2015). *Carbon capitalism: Energy, social reproduction and world order*. Roman & Littlefield.

Dodge, J., & Metze, T. (2017). Hydraulic fracturing as an interpretive policy problem: Lessons on energy controversies in Europe and the U.S.A. *Journal of Environmental Policy & Planning, 19*(1), 1–13, https://doi.org/10.1080/1523908X.2016.1277947

Dusyk, N., Axsen, J., & Dullemond, K. (2018). Who cares about climate change? The mass media and socio-political acceptance of Canada's oil sands and northern gateway pipeline. *Energy Research & Social Science, 37*, 12–21. https://doi.org/10.1016/j.erss.2017.07.005

Edge, M. (2016). The never-ending story: Postmedia, the competition bureau, and press ownership concentration in Canada. *Canadian Journal of Media Studies, Spring/Summer 2016*, 53–81

Endres, D. E., Cozen, B., Trey Barnett, J., O'Byrne, M., & Rai Peterson, T. (2016). Communicating energy in a climate (of) crisis. *Annals of the International Communication Association, 40*, 419–447. https://doi.org/10.1080/23808985.2015.1173 5267

Fast, T. (2014). Stapled to the front door: Neoliberal extractivism in Canada. *Studies in Political Economy, 94*(3), 31–60. https://doi.org/10.1080/19187033.2014.11674953

Fitz-Morris, J. (2015, April 14). Tom Mulcair's 'Dutch disease' diagnosis was poor politics, but sound economics. *CBC News.* www.cbc.ca/news

Forster, J. B., & Clark, B. (2012, December 01). The planetary emergency. *Monthly Review.* www.monthlyreview.org

Friedel, T. L. (2008). (Not so) crude text and images: Staging native in 'big oil' advertising. *Visual Studies, 23*(3), 238–254. https://doi.org/10.1080/14725860802489908

Gollom, M. (2012, May 18). Is Canada suffering from 'Dutch disease'? *CBC News.* www.cbc.ca/news

Gray-Donald, D. (2018, August 13). What Canada's major media are forgetting when they report on oil. *The Narwhal.* https://thenarwhal.ca/oil-projections-climate-change/

Gunster, S., & Saurette, P. (2014). Storylines in the Sands: News, Narrative, and Ideology in the Calgary Herald. *Canadian Journal of Communication, 39*(3), 333–359. https://doi.org/10.22230/cjc.2014v39n3a2830

Gunton, T. (2014). Staple theory and the new staple boom. In J. Stanford (Ed.), *The staple theory @ 50* (pp. 43–82). Canadian Centre for Policy Alternatives.

Hackett, R. A., Forde, S., Gunster, S., & Foxwell-Norton, K. (2017). *Journalism and climate crisis: Public engagement, media alternatives.* Routledge.

Harvey, D. (2007). *A brief history of neoliberalism.* Oxford University Press.

Harvey, D. (2011). *The enigma of capital and the crises of capitalism.* Oxford University Press.

Honarvar, A., Rozhon, J., Millington, D., Walden, T., Murillo, C. A., & Walden, Z. (2011). *Economic impacts of new oil sands projects in Alberta (2010–2035).* Canadian Energy Research Institute and University of Calgary. www.api.org

Huber, M. (2013). *Lifeblood: Oil, freedom, and the forces of capital.* University of Minnesota Press.

Innis, H. A. (1956). *The fur trade in Canada: An introduction to Canadian economic history.* University of Toronto Press.

Intergovernmental Panel on Climate Change. (2022). *Climate change 2022: Impacts, adaptation and vulnerability.* www.ipcc.ch/report/sixth-assessment-report-working-group-ii/

Karl, T. L. (1997). *The paradox of plenty: Oil booms and Petro-states.* University of California Press.

Kennedy, E. (2014). From Petro-states to 'new realities': Perspectives on the geographies of oil. *Geography Compass, 8*(4), 262–276. https://doi.org/10.1111/gec3.12127

Klein, N. (2014). *This changes everything: Capitalism vs. the climate.* Simon & Schuster.

Kojola, E. (2017). (re)constructing the pipeline: Workers, environmentalists and ideology in media coverage of the keystone XL pipeline. *Critical Sociology, 43*(6), 893917. https://doi.org/10.1177/0896920515598564

Lee, M. (2014). LNG: British Columbia's quest for a new staple industry. In J. Stanford (Ed.), *The staple theory @ 50* (pp. 80–83). Canadian Centre for Policy Alternatives.

Levant, E. (2010). *Ethical oil: The case for Canada's oil sands.* McClelland & Stewart.

MacNeil, R. (2014). The decline of Canadian environmental regulation: Neoliberalism and the staples bias. *Studies in Political Economy, 93*(1), 81–106. https://doi.org/10.1080/19187033.2014.11674965

Malm, A. (2013). The origins of fossil capital: From water to steam in the British cotton industry. *Historical Materialism, 21*(1), 15–68. https://doi.org/10.1163/1569206X-12341279

Matthews, R. (2014). Committing more Canadian sociology: Response to the comments on "Committing Canadian sociology". *Canadian Review of Sociology/Revue Canadienne De Sociologie, 51*(4), 409–417.

McNally, D. (2011). *Global slump: The economics and politics of crisis and resistance.* Fernwood Publishing.

Meadows, D. H. [and others] (1972). *The limits to growth: A report for the Club of Rome's project on the predicament of mankind.* Universe Books.

Metze, T. (2017). Fracking the debate: Frame shifts and boundary work in Dutch decision making on shale gas. *Journal of Environmental Policy & Planning, 19*(1), 35–52, https://doi.org/10.1080/1523908X.2014.941462

Mitchell, T. (2009). Carbon democracy. *Economy and Society, 38*(3), 399–432. https://doi.org/10.1080/03085140903020598

Neubauer, R. (2018). Moving beyond the petrostate: Northern gateway, extractivism, and the Canadian petrobloc. *Studies in Political Economy, 99*(3), 246–267. https://doi.org/10.1080/07078552.2018.1536369

Newman, N. (2011). *Mainstream media and the distribution of news in the age of social discovery.* Reuters Institute for the Study of Journalism, University of Oxford. http://reutersinstitute.politics.ox.ac.uk/

Nikiforuk, A. (2010). *Tar sands: Dirty oil and the future of a continent.* Greystone Books Ltd.

Olive, A., & Delshad, A. B. (2017). Fracking and framing: A comparative analysis of media coverage of hydraulic fracturing in Canadian and U.S. newspapers. *Environmental Communication, 11*(6), 784–799. https://doi.org/10.1080/17524032.2016.1275734

Papineau, J. W., & Deacon, L. (2017). Fort McMurray and the Canadian oil sands: Local coverage of national importance. *Environmental Communication, 11*(5), 593–608. https://doi.org/10.1080/17524032.2017.1289107

Pineault, É. (2016, May 13). Welcome to the age of extractivism and extreme oil. *The National Observer.* www.nationalobserver.com

Pineault, É. (2018). The capitalist pressure to extract: The ecological and political economy of extreme oil in Canada. *Studies in Political Economy, 99*(2), 130–150. https://doi.org/10.1080/07078552.2018.1492063

Podobnik, B. (2006). *Global energy shifts: Fostering sustainability in a turbulent age.* Temple University Press.

Preston, J. (2017). Racial extractivism and white settler colonialism: An examination of the Canadian Tar Sands mega-projects. *Cultural Studies, 31*(2–3), 353–375. https://doi.org/10.1080/09502386.2017.1303432

Raso, K., & Neubauer, R. J. (2016). Managing dissent: Energy pipelines and 'new right' politics in Canada. *Canadian Journal of Communication, 41*(1), 115–133. https://doi.org/10.22230/cjc2016v41n1a2777

Remillard, C. (2011). Picturing environmental risk: The Canadian oil sands and the national geographic. *International Communication Gazette, 73*(1–2), 127–143. https://doi.org/10.1177/1748048510386745

Schumacher, E. (1973). *Small is beautiful: Economics as if people mattered.* Harper & Row.

Smil, V. (2017). *Energy transitions: Global and national perspectives* (2nd ed.). Praeger.

Smythe, D. W. (1981). *Dependency road: Communications, capitalism, consciousness and Canada.* Ablex Publishing Corp.

Stoddart, M. C. J., Tindall, D. B., Smith, J., & Haluza-Delay, R. (2017). Media access and political efficacy in the eco-politics of climate change: Canadian national news and mediated policy networks. *Environmental Communication, 11*(3), 386–400. https://doi.org/10.1080/17524032.2016.1275731

Svampa, M. (2015). Commodities consensus: Neoextractivism and enclosure of the commons in Latin America. *South Atlantic Quarterly, 114*(1), 65–82. https://doi.org/10.1215/00382876-2831290

Szeman, I. (2013). How to know about oil: Energy epistemologies and political futures. *Journal of Canadian Studies, 47*(3), 145–168.

Takach, G. (2013). Selling nature in a resource-based economy: Romantic/extractive gazes and Alberta's bituminous sands. *Environmental Communication, 7*(2), 211–230. https://doi.org/10.1080/17524032.2013.778208

Tindall, D. B. (2014). A distinctive Canadian sociology? *Canadian Review of Sociology/Revue Canadienne De Sociologie, 51*(4), 395–401. https://doi.org/10.1111/cars.12054

Urry, J. (2013). *Societies beyond oil: Oil dregs and social futures.* Zed Books.

Urry, J. (2014). The problem of energy. *Theory, Culture & Society, 31*(5), 3–20.

Veltmeyer, H., & Bowles, P. (2014). Extractivist resistance: The case of the Enbridge oil pipeline project in Northern British Columbia. *The Extractive Industries and Society, 1*(1), 59–68.

Watkins, M. H. (1963). A staple theory of economic growth. *Canadian Journal of Economics and Political Science, 29*(2), 141–158. https://doi.org/10.2307/139461

Watkins, M. H. (2007). Comment: Staples redux. *Studies in Political Economy, 79*(1), 213–226. https://doi.org/10.1080/19187033.2007.11675098

Way, L. (2011). An energy superpower or a super sales pitch? Building the case through an examination of Canadian newspapers coverage of oil sands. *Canadian Political Science Review, 5*(1), 74–98.

Wilkinson, R. G. (1973). *Poverty and progress: An ecological model of economic development.* Methuen Publishing.

Wilson, S. Szeman, I., & Carlson, A. (2017). On petrocultures: Or, why we need to understand oil to understand everything else. In S. Wilson, I. Szeman, & A. Carlson (Eds.), *Petrocultures: Oil, politics, culture* (pp. 3–19). McGillQueen's Press.

Winseck, D. (2019). *Media and Internet concentration in Canada, 1984–2018.* www.cmcrp.org

Wood, T. (2018). Energy's citizens: The making of a Canadian Petro-public. *Canadian Journal of Communication, 43*(1), 75–92.

Wrigley, E. A. (2010). *Energy and the English industrial revolution.* Cambridge University Press.

3   Shale Gas and Global LNG Trade

The Intergovernmental Panel on Climate Change has repeatedly emphasized in its recent reports (2022a, 2022b) that the urgency of climate change mitigation and adaptation necessitates a rapid expansion of renewable energy sources. Nonetheless, given how seamlessly fossil fuels have been integrated into everyday life, many energy policy scholars (e.g., Babaee & Loughlin, 2018; Brauers, 2022; Smil, 2015, 2017) have expressed concern that the pace of an energy transition to renewables will be slow and that a more probable transition in the coming decades will involve the gradual displacement of coal and possibly crude oil by natural gas.

For a long time, natural gas has received significantly less public attention than coal and crude oil (Smil, 2015). On the one hand, this is due to the invisibility of natural gas, which produces no odor or taste when burned and is transported to homes through underground pipelines. On the other hand, the sheer abundance of natural gas contributes to its low profile: despite occasional price and availability fluctuations on global markets, there has never been a natural gas crisis comparable to the oil shocks of the 1970s. Russia is the only major gas exporter that has repeatedly used its gas supply to Europe as political leverage in recent decades.

That being said, it is concerning that the world's dependence on natural gas is soaring. In many countries, natural gas has already supplanted coal as the second most important energy source after crude oil. The increasing importance of natural gas in the global energy mix is driven by the rapid growth of its use in industrial fertilizer production, household heating and cooking, transportation, and, most importantly, electricity generation. In addition, governments, energy corporations, and even some environmental organizations have branded natural gas as a "bridge fuel" that facilitates the world's transition to renewable energy sources, thereby contributing to its increased publicity (Brauers, 2022; Klein, 2014). Such is the context in which the British Columbia (BC) Liberal government announced its ambitious plan for liquefied natural gas (LNG) exports in late 2011.

This chapter presents a historical and contextual overview of BC LNG. It sheds light on how the US shale gas boom, in combination with Asian

DOI: 10.4324/9781003350620-3

countries' strong gas demands, inspired British Columbia to aggressively pursue LNG exports. Moreover, the enduring potency of LNG in British Columbia's political economy becomes apparent when examined from a historical perspective. The promotion of LNG exports since late 2011 was actually British Columbia's third attempt to launch an LNG industry. This necessitates an examination of the past to explain why discussions about BC LNG resurfaced in late 2011 and grew into a high-profile controversy in later years.

Shortly, I begin by examining the global shale gas boom since the early 2000s and its relevant public narratives. The following sections then reconstruct the timeline of BC LNG, tracing its origin back to the failed West Coast LNG proposal during the early 1980s. The chapter's analysis explicates that the hype surrounding BC LNG exports to Asia since late 2011 must be understood as a continuation of previous unsuccessful attempts to secure additional trade partners for Canadian staples. It is also driven by carbon-intensive capitalist reproduction's push for sustaining the established global political economic order.

3.1. The Shale Gas Boom

The fossil fuel described as "natural gas" in daily language consists almost entirely of methane, plus small amounts of other chemical compounds in the alkane series, notably ethane (C_2H_6), propane (C_3H_8), butane (C_4H_{10}), and pentane (C_5H_{12}). When compared with other fossil fuels, natural gas has three notable advantages. First, its gas format offers high combustion efficiency. In the electricity industry, the combination of gas and steam turbines is the most efficient solution of energy conversion currently available. Second, the burning of pure methane – the primary component of natural gas – only generates water and CO_2, making it the cleanest fossil fuel in terms of combustion. Third, after high initial investment in pipeline construction, the transportation of natural gas is comparatively cost-effective.

In terms of the major disadvantages of natural gas, the first is the risk of leakage during extraction and transportation, which has already posed a significant threat to the global climate system. As a greenhouse gas (GHG), methane is "more than 25 times as potent as carbon dioxide at trapping heat in the atmosphere" (United States Environmental Protection Agency, 2022, para. 2). A recent study (Hmiel et al., 2020) published by *Nature* found that methane emissions from fossil fuel extraction have been underestimated up to 40%, which means the natural gas industry has a much bigger carbon footprint than previous estimates. The second disadvantage is the lower energy density of natural gas compared to petroleum products. The average higher heating value (HHV) of liquid fuels is three orders of magnitude higher than natural gas (Smil, 2015). A common method to improve the energy density of natural gas is liquefaction: at $-160\ °C$, natural gas turns into a liquid with a significantly improved HHV (roughly 600 times the value for typical natural gas). LNG shipment via tankers is also the only cost-effective way to transport natural gas across oceans due to the technical difficulty of constructing pipelines in deep water.

Conventional oil and gas production are interconnected since a substantial amount of natural gas must be injected back into nearby oil deposits to maintain the minimum pressure required for oil extraction. Accordingly, early estimates of global natural gas supplies, derived from the "peak oil" model, predicted that the global natural gas industry would continue to expand until 2025 and then sharply decline after 2045 (Campbell, 2005). Nevertheless, this timeline has been overhauled in recent years due to the worldwide proliferation of gas extraction from shale formations.

Shale gas refers to methane deposits within shale rock formations. This unconventional type of gas reserves was not economically obtainable until the early 2000s, when the low permeability of shale was solved by innovations in drilling technologies, namely the combination of hydraulic fracturing and horizontal drilling (hereafter referred to as "fracking"). Unlike conventional extraction methods that remove oil from pools embedded in impermeable rock layers, fracking allows the separation of both oil and natural gas from deep rock formations themselves (Montgomery & Smith, 2010). A typical fracking operation begins with a well drilled from the surface to a subsurface location above the target shale layer. Precise drilling is implemented horizontally along the shale layer's contour. Finally, a highly pressured mixture of water, sand, and chemicals is injected into the shale layer to crack it, which forces natural gas to migrate to the well.

Since the late 2000s, there has been a global "shale gas boom" as a result of the significant increase in estimated recoverable gas due to fracking. Take North America as an example. The United States has approximately 7.7 trillion m^3 of conventional natural gas reserves, but the application of fracking has boosted its technically recoverable gas reserves to a total of 24.4 trillion m^3 (Howarth et al., 2011). For Canada, the numbers are 1.8 and 11 trillion m^3, respectively. As a result of the shale gas boom, updated estimates now suggest that the world may not reach the peak of gas production around 2050 or even 2070 (Smil, 2015). As the world is running out of easy-to-exploit fossil fuels, the abundance of remaining shale gas reserves makes it an ideal candidate to be the next dominant fuel of human civilization.

Along with the expansion of fracking for shale gas, international gas exports have been increasingly facilitated through LNG pipelines and tankers. In 2016, a total of 258 million tons (MT) of LNG was traded, more than twice the volume of shipments in 2000 (International Gas Union, 2017). Despite such rapid growth, LNG remains a peripheral sector in the global energy landscape (Smil, 2015, 2017; Wood, 2012), with its further expansion being constrained by its cost relative to other fossil fuels as well as very high initial infrastructure costs (e.g., the construction of liquefaction plants, special tankers, regasification terminals, adjacent pipelines, etc.). Today, LNG supplies significant portions of primary energy in Japan, South Korea, and Taiwan, but elsewhere it remains marginal, with market shares dwarfed by crude oil and coal.

Recently, the global LNG trade has been influenced by two notable trends. First, growing energy consumption driven by Asian economic development is expected to be the primary driver of future LNG production growth (International Gas Union, 2017). Mainland China began to import LNG only in 2006, but in just a few years, it surpassed South Korea to become the world's third largest LNG importer. India currently imports 19.2 MT (ranked fourth in the world). Both countries have plenty of room for LNG to displace coal for household heating and electricity generation. Second, the shale gas boom has fundamentally changed the supply-demand order of the North American natural gas system. With an average of 35,000 new fracking wells appearing in the United States every year, the country's shale gas production grew from virtually nothing to more than 0.85 billion m^3 per day between 2000 and 2013 (Medlock et al., 2014). As North America was flooded by excessive shale gas, the region's natural gas prices collapsed. Between 2010 and 2015, Henry Hub spot natural gas prices (North America's benchmark prices) rarely rose beyond $5 USD/MBtu. In contrast, during the same period, natural gas prices in Asia stayed above $10 USD/MBtu. This notable price gap prompted increasing interests amongst investors and policymakers in exporting North America's oversupplied shale gas to Asian markets. It was in this context that the provincial government of British Columbia joined the global LNG race in late 2011.

Despite the enormous economic potential of fracking, it has been strongly opposed by residents living in fracking zones and environmentalists due to the following environmental concerns. First and foremost, fracking is an extremely hydro-intensive process and a serious threat to drinking water safety. Whilst conventional oil wells require approximately 60,000 gallons of water, a fracking well requires between 2 and 9 million gallons of water (Harden-Donahue, 2011; Wylie, 2018). Furthermore, the opening of shale formation is achieved with the use of chemicals and proppant. FracFocus (n.d.), a corporative website maintained by US state water officials and the Interstate Oil and Gas Compact Commission, lists 59 chemicals commonly used in fracking, but many "patented" chemicals are hidden from public awareness and pose significant threat to underground water and people living near to fracking wells. Increasing seismic risk is another focal point of fracking-related public discussions. Central Oklahoma is a representative case, where scientific investigations have directly linked a sharp increase of earthquakes to massive fracking activities (e.g., Keranen et al., 2014).

Most crucially, when compared with conventional natural gas production, fracking dramatically increases the severity of methane leakage. According to

Howarth et al.'s (2011) estimate, "methane emissions [from fracking] are at least 30% more than and perhaps more than twice as great as those from conventional gas" (p. 679). Considering that there are nearly 2.5 million fracked wells worldwide, with the United States having 1.1 million of them (Montgomery & Smith, 2010), the amount of methane leaking from these wells completely offsets the moderate environmental benefits of burning natural gas instead of coal. Thus, critics of fracking (e.g., Howarth, 2014; Nikiforuk, 2015) have deemed shale gas as a serious threat to climate change mitigation. In addition, the continual growth of natural gas usage would weaken the desire to develop renewables, further delaying the progress of transforming the world's economy into a post-carbon one (Healey & Jaccard, 2016).

3.2. Public Communication of Fracking

Despite the aforementioned environmental concerns, the fossil fuel industry still advocates shale gas as a revolutionary opportunity too valuable to lose and urges further deregulation for fracking practices. In her investigation into the impact of fracking in the United States, Wylie (2018) found that corporate lobbying for fracking's regulatory exemptions is primarily responsible for the reckless shale gas boom. From a rhetorical perspective, two claims are at the center of shale gas propaganda. First, energy conglomerates and some government regulators make the case that fracking is a mature drilling technique with decades of proven safety records. Nevertheless, an inquiry into this proposition reveals its inaccuracy. Although the United States Department of Energy had demonstrated the viability of massive-scale fracking during the 1970s, it was not widely recognized by producers until 1998, when George Mitchell, a Texas oilman, found means to significantly lower the average cost of a fracking operation (Wylie, 2018). Thus, it is only in the last decade or two that fracking has become widespread as a means of facilitating the extraction of natural gas.

Another claim pervading concerted government and industry propaganda promoting the shale gas boom is the proposal of natural gas as a "bridge fuel" in the transition to low-carbon and eventually renewable energy systems. In both North America and Europe, government and industry stakeholders have aggressively branded shale gas as a "clean fuel" compatible with climate change mitigation (see Bomberg, 2017; Dodge & Lee, 2017; Metze, 2017). The prevalence of the "bridge fuel" concept in public narratives has been critically scrutinized in scholarly discussions. Focusing on the case of BC LNG, Stephenson and her colleagues (2012) reviewed best available empirical evidence on the climate impacts of shale gas and concluded that it is highly problematic to consider shale gas as clean energy source because factors influencing its lifecycle emissions are "poorly characterized and remain contested in the academic literature" (p. 452). A recent report by Oil Change

International (Stockman et al., 2019) reached a similar conclusion that "the myth of gas as a 'bridge' to a stable climate does not stand up to scrutiny" (p. 18). In short, although shale gas is promoted as a better alternative to coal and oil, it is by no means a bridge fuel that facilitates the decarbonization of the global economy.

With respect to media coverage, before 2010, discussions on shale gas and fracking had been largely confined to the fossil fuel industry's trade publications and mainstream media's business sections, without much controversy. As found in several chronological accounts (e.g., Matthews & Hansen, 2018; Mazur, 2016, 2018), the controversy over fracking grew rapidly between 2010 and 2011, first in the United States and then internationally. According to Mazur (2016), two high-profile events played crucial roles in drawing public attention to fracking's environmental impacts. The first was the acclaimed anti-fracking documentary *Gasland* (Fox, 2010), which grabbed public attention with horrifying images of tainted aquifers and ignitable drinking water. The second was the offshore Deepwater Horizon disaster in April 2010, which spurred prolific media coverage on the potential risks underlying rapidly growing US oil and gas production. According to Mazur's (2018) analysis of fracking's presence in British, German, and US news coverage, media attention to anti-fracking activism peaked during 2012–2014, with the *New York Times* being "the most potent agenda-setting news organization in the United States and also important internationally" (p. 538). US media attention to fracking dropped after 2014, partly because the New York state banned fracking in 2014, and the *New York Times* reduced its corresponding coverage. Yet, the public contests on fracking was far from over due to the spread of fracking activities into other countries like Canada.

As fracking turned into a complicated and controversial issue for policymakers and other relevant stakeholders, the growing public awareness of it encountered conflicting stakeholder opinions, expert claims, and news reports. Echoing other environmental controversies, public contests over fracking are value-driven conflicts wherein a wide range of stakeholders seek to negotiate the public meanings of fracking through the framing of facts and counter-facts. Consequently, the public interpret uncertainties about fracking in conflicting ways. As found in public surveys conducted in the United States (Evensen & Stedman, 2017) and Britain (Howell, 2018), respondents held polarized views on fracking, and more importantly, their general values and beliefs – such as those about environmental protection, local community, and political identification – precede the formation of their specific attitudes toward fracking. In other words, increasing the public's knowledge about fracking has little impacts on their beliefs about shale gas developments.

Therefore, fracking is not purely a technological problem which can be resolved with more scientific analysis; it is also a communicative problem which consists of definitional and interpretive struggles (Matthews & Hansen, 2018; Metze & Dodge, 2016) and challenges the "information deficit" model

(Kollmuss & Agyeman, 2002) following by many policymakers. Political ideology and party affiliation are becoming notable factors in public perceptions of the relationship between fracking and climate change. For instance, a US national survey conducted by Boudet and her colleagues (2014) revealed that people who hold egalitarian worldviews and associate fracking primarily with environmental impacts tend to oppose the process. By contrast, people who are politically conservative and associate fracking primarily with the economy and energy security tend to support it.

The politicization of fracking points to the social acceptance literature's concern about the sociopolitical acceptance of energy policies (Gaede & Rowlands, 2018; Wolsink, 2018; Wüstenhagen et al., 2007). The concept of social acceptance addresses factors influencing the implementation of energy policies, especially those related to the development of energy infrastructure. In the words of Wolsink (2018), one of the leading experts in this field, "social acceptance should be understood as a bundle of processes of decision-making on issues concerning the promotion of – or counteraction against – new phenomena and new elements in the transformation of current energy systems" (p. 287). According to the typology by Wüstenhagen et al. (2007), there are three dimensions of the concept (1) sociopolitical acceptance, (2) community acceptance, and (3) market acceptance. In the case of fracking, community acceptance, which refers to the consent of local stakeholders near energy projects, has been recognized as the most pivotal dimension. For instance, drawing upon survey and interview results, Darrick Evensen and his colleagues (Evensen & Brown-Steiner, 2018; Evensen & Stedman, 2017, 2018) found that public opinion about fracking is affected more by fracking-related benefits and risks to community "good life" than shale gas development's association with climate change. Another survey (Yu et al., 2018) conducted in China also found similar tendencies. Taken together, the social acceptance of fracking depends less on knowledge about impacts. The issue's contentious nature often compromises the trustworthiness of expert information. Accordingly, what became pivotal for public deliberation are communications "focusing on the shared historical and cultural experiences that shape values and general beliefs" (Evensen & Stedman, 2017, p. 18).

In communication and media studies, recent research on fracking communications has focussed on how their intensifying politicization is shaped by each country's political and economic context and respective discursive dynamics. For instance, Metze's (2017) analysis of shale gas debates in the Netherlands has demonstrated how the transformation of public understanding of fracking from an acceptable drilling practice to an alarming environmental threat hinged on the discursive strategies adopted by opponents, which emphasized the many uncertainties underlying fracking's economic benefits and environmental impacts. Driven by such a shift in public understanding, the Dutch government took a cautious approach and issued policies that frame fracking as a planning issue. Like the Netherlands case, by expanding the scope of fracking conversations, environmental organizations and concerned citizens in New York and the UK effectively challenged the "economic opportunity" storyline used by fracking advocates (Bomberg, 2017; Dodge & Lee, 2017).

Notably, opponents' interpretation of fracking in relation to public health and local democracy issues opened alternative discursive spaces to accommodate citizens' own experiences and voices. Admittedly, not all struggles against fracking have enjoyed the same level of success. In Poland and Germany, fracking initiatives were supported by regulatory relief and tax incentives, and the public momentum of such policy support was primarily maintained by government actors' promotion of "scientific dialogues" on fracking (Bigl, 2017; Bornemann, 2017; Lis & Stankiewicz, 2017). Most of these dialogues were sponsored by the private sector and disproportionally highlighted expert opinions favorable to the pro-fracking side. By branding such expert opinions as "objective claims", political and business elites managed to frame fracking as crucial to securing a future energy supply, thereby closing down other viable interpretations by citizens' voices.

Overall, the reviewed cases collectively demonstrate that fracking presents an interpretive problem interweaving economic, energy, and environmental factors at national and transnational levels. It could be viewed as an emblematic problem consisting of two central tensions: the classic tension between economic growth and environmental protection as well as the escalating tension between the urgency of post-carbon transition and the pertinacity of fossil fuel consumption (Dodge & Metze, 2017).

Despite the presence of both tensions across countries, media framing and the political responses they receive can be quite different from case to case since stakeholder interventions can either open up or close down certain ways of understanding fracking. Amongst the various discursive spaces where stakeholders intervene, the media sphere, consisting of both legacy outlets and social media platforms, is a crucial one. Studies on fracking coverage suggest that relevant media coverage is informed by a sense of contest which corresponds to the contrasting opinions of different interested stakeholder groups (Matthews & Hansen, 2018). For news stories depicting fracking as an "economic good", popular topics tend to address job creation, regional investment, and, for European countries particularly, less dependence on unethical energy from Russia and the Middle East. In some cases, geopolitical concerns are more effective than economic factors in mobilizing public support for fracking. Bigl's (2017) analysis of fracking stories in the German press has found that the potential challenge of securing Germany's energy supply against the backdrop of the Crimean crisis plays a central role in the construction of unbalanced reporting, with the risks associated with fracking being mostly ignored.

Meanwhile, news stories depicting fracking as an "environmental concern" tend to discuss topics such as underground water contamination and its subsequent threat to public health. Led by the wide circulation of strong anti-fracking sentiment in *Gasland* (Fox, 2010), water quality has become the most publicized environmental risk of fracking in both North America and Europe (Jaspal & Nerlich, 2014; Olive & Delshad, 2017). It should be noted that many news reports on fracking have presented its economic and environmental perspectives as a dichotomy. Readers may learn about fracking as either an economic issue or an environmental issue, but it is rare to see opinion pieces discussing both perspectives comprehensively.

Concerning factors underlying the media's framing of fracking, previous research has addressed variations found in the reporting of fracking's benefits and risks in relation to the ideological stances and socio-political contexts of journalists' news organizations. Focusing on UK media coverage, Jaspal and Nerlich (2014) have identified an unfolding debate between left-leaning and right-leaning outlets, with the former side's skeptical stance having the upper hand at the time of the study. One insightful observation from their analysis is the important role played by "threat positioning" in the mediated process of fracking deliberation. Whilst left-leaning outlets addressed fracking mainly as a multi-faceted threat to human beings and the environment, right-leaning outlets also used the notion of "threat" but in relation to a different target: the UK's economic future. They appealed to the scarcity of energy sources and criticized the high cost of renewable energy to portray anti-fracking activities as threatening. Thus, inherently vague notions such as people's desire for security and prosperity could be used as mobilizing factors on both sides of the fracking controversy.

Amongst these competing notions, the most contested one is arguably transition, which is closely related to the "bridge fuel" designation of shale gas. Depending on one's perception of fossil fuels, shale gas could be considered either a facilitator of or a barrier to reduction in GHG emissions. Unlike traditional risk management models which evaluate the environment from the perspective of cost-benefit analysis, debating shale gas in the broad picture of post-carbon transition opens the realm of normative and ideological conflicts (Dodge & Metze, 2017; Fischer, 2003).

Sociopolitical contexts that underpin domestic media discussions on fracking often create certain focal points for media attention. In North America, for instance, although both Canadian and US newspapers have prioritized the issue of water quality in their coverage of fracking, beyond this common concern, there are noticeable differences in media focusses (Olive & Delshad, 2017). Compared to their US counterparts, the Canadian media tend to focus more on fracking's benefits to a local economy but less on its potential harm to wildlife. Such national variations are even more prominent in Europe due to the region's complex energy supply and consumption dynamics.

In terms of the information subsidies offered by both pro-fracking and anti-fracking actors, one question frequently appears in previous research: which side is more effective at influencing media messages? Although fracking opponents have been successful in several places such as New York, Britain, and the Netherlands, there is emerging evidence pointing to a reciprocal relationship between the business sector and news outlets. Because news production is constrained by general journalistic routines and practices, fracking reporting tends to proportionally favor business and political elites as authoritative and credible sources of news (Matthews & Hansen, 2018). Consequently, the agenda-building efforts of fracking opponents are repeatedly met with discrimination and exclusion. Even in cases wherein anti-fracking actors' arguments prevail and eventually contribute to moratoria on fracking, this is often caused by high-profile environmental accidents, which trigger the crisis frame of news production and temporarily drive media attention towards environmental concerns. For instance, in Jaspal and Nerlich's (2014) analysis of the UK press, an important background story on which fracking opponents constructed their narratives was seismic activity in Lancashire.

Nevertheless, not all risks associated with fracking are easily visible for public scrutiny. Thus, the "jobs versus environment" dichotomy, around which many anti-fracking activists in the United States and Europe have built their arguments (Matthews & Hansen, 2018), has inherent limits. Accordingly, a key issue this dissertation explores is how to transcend that dichotomy and develop better arguments to counter the celebration of the omnipresence of fossil fuels, which has been used as a central discursive strategy by fracking proponents.

In sum, the industrial production and transportation of fossil fuels always pose a threat to public health and safety and damage the environment. However, before the rise of extreme carbon, these drawbacks tended to evoke a relatively low level of public opposition so long as the daily operations of energy production proceeded normally. Occasionally, serious accidents could draw public scrutiny to the energy sector and expose the flaws in its regulations, but for the most part, such accidents are often addressed as anomalies, with blame attributed only to the responsible persons or companies instead of being linked to environmental concerns such as sustainable development, energy transition, and climate change (Matthews & Hansen, 2018). Consequently, public anger over the energy sector's misconduct often calms down as time passes by, which reflects the event-led character of the 24-hour news cycle and the constraints such a cycle imposes on environmental reporting.

Thus, environmental concerns alone could not explain the notable LNG opposition in the BC public sphere from 2011 to 2017, when the sector remained a "castle in the air". One theory could be the worldwide proliferation of anti-fracking movements accounting for such sustained public attention. However, in his analysis of the evolvement of the fracking controversy in the United States from 2010 to 2012, Mazur (2016) has identified three interrelated trends contributing to the issue's prevalence: (1) the success of the anti-fracking documentary *Gasland* and its introduction of fracking to public awareness,

(2) the steady growth of media coverage on the potential risks underlying rapidly expanding shale gas production in the United States (especially the ten-part series report "Drilling Down" by the *New York Times*), which stemmed from growing public concern as well as the aftermath of the Deepwater Horizon oil spill, and (3) consistent local opposition against fracking when shale gas producers attempted to expand their operations into Pennsylvania and New York State. Mazur (2016) has also argued that given the US media's leading role in international reportage, their continuing attention to fracking further spread to other nations where fracking is potentially applicable. If one accepts this argument, then the case of BC LNG is a successor of the momentum built in the United States.

As later chapters will discuss, however, the BC LNG case should not be simply interpreted as a copycat merely following the playbook written by US fracking opponents. Although both proponents and opponents of BC LNG have made frequent references to the ongoing "US shale gas revolution", the most direct cause of the case's sudden elevation in Canadian mainstream media was the BC Liberal Party's framing of it as the party's central economic platform during the months leading to the 2013 BC provincial election. Whilst the public contestations over fracking across several US states could be viewed as a gradual politicization process brought by increasing media coverage, BC LNG was born with strong political sentiment. As discussed in the introductory chapter, British Columbia's unique contextual factors further complicate the discursive dynamics surrounding shale gas production and LNG exports.

3.3. 1980–2010: British Columbia's Early Attempts to Establish a LNG Sector

On October 28, 1980, the *Globe and Mail* (French, 1980 October 28) reported a preliminary agreement reached between Dome (a Calgary-based energy corporation) and a consortium of five Japanese utilities. The agreement focussed on establishing LNG exports from Western Canada to Japan. Regarding the agreement's significance, Dome's president, William Richards, asserted that Japan's thriving natural gas market would offer great potential for the future growth of the Canadian natural gas sector, thereby addressing the challenge of overproduction experienced by many domestic producers. He also stated that the agreement would benefit Canada's shipbuilding industry since some of the LNG carriers included in the agreement's transportation section would be open to Canadian bidders. The story briefly mentioned that the project's progress might be delayed by federal–provincial coordination over taxation or resistance from environmental activists, yet such hurdles, the story insisted, would be overcome since the agreement, especially Canadian interests in it, had ensured government support from both provincial and federal levels.

This news item was the first mention of exporting BC natural gas to Asia contained in the ProQuest Canadian Newsstream database. At that time, long-distance LNG shipment was a fledging sector. However, Dome's attempt did not come as a surprise to fellow Canadian gas producers, for whom reaching out to Asian customers had become a high priority since the stagnating North American gas market was unable to absorb excessive natural gas produced by expanding drilling activities in Western Canada. Japan seemed to be an ideal candidate with a booming economy sustaining its domination in global LNG imports. Following Dome's announcement, Petro-Canada (in those years, a crown corporation) and Carter Energy (a Vancouver-based independent energy producer) also joined the competition with their own LNG terminal proposals targeting Japan.

The momentum of BC natural gas kept growing and peaked in March 1982, when ten major gas-use proposals – in the categories of natural gas liquefaction, ethylene-based petrochemicals, and methanol and fertilizers – competed for the BC government's approval (Sigurdson, 1982 March 8). Although an earlier estimate by George Govier had increased estimates of British Columbia's explorable natural gas to 25 trillion cubic feet (Sigurdson, 1982 March 4), it was determined that the province's supply and demand could only accommodate the production capacity of a single LNG plant. The BC government eventually picked Dome's West Coast LNG proposal since it promised to provide the highest royalty return and was backed by the preliminary agreement.

Shortly after receiving governmental support, however, the project was hit by a series of unfavorable developments. During the project's public hearings at the National Energy Board (NEB), evidence emerged that, within the Japanese consortium spearheading the project, only NIC Resources was firmly committed to Dome's plan ("LNG accord with Japanese felt uncertain", 1982 August 26). The extent to which the project would prioritize national interest also became a matter of debate as Dome explained that its Canadian content, such as construction contracts and operating labor, might only reach a threshold of 60% ("Canadian content of LNG plan by Dome Pete may be only 60%", 1982 November 2). In 1983, falling LNG prices on the Japanese side further challenged the project's business viability and strengthened the Japanese consortium's unwillingness to guarantee financing (Sigurdson, 1983 April 26).

Under these circumstances, Dome was forced to postpone public hearings at the NEB and renegotiate with the Japanese consortium. Consequently, the planned construction of West Coast LNG entered a yearlong delay, which significantly damaged stakeholder confidence (Taylor, 1984 February 28). In November 1984, the project was taken over by Canada LNG Corporation, founded as a joint venture representing a consortium of eight Canadian energy companies led by Petro-Canada and Mobil Oil of Canada (Kevin, 1985 March 19; Lush, 1984 October 31). Dome ended up as a minor stakeholder within the consortium. Seeking to salvage the project, the Canadian consortium attempted several rounds of negotiation with its Japanese counterpart throughout 1985. Such efforts ultimately failed, and the project was cancelled in January 1986.

The West Coast LNG case revealed several factors constraining the overseas expansion of BC natural gas exports, and, to a large extent, these factors remained when the BC Liberal Party revived the LNG dream in late 2011. First, as shown in the negotiations between the Canadian and Japanese consortiums, the business prospect of exporting BC LNG to Asia is highly sensitive to international market conditions. The high initial costs of establishing LNG infrastructure in BC, as well as fluctuations in natural gas prices in Asian markets, impose significant economic challenges. When the Canadian and Japanese consortiums entered their final negotiation, the *Globe and Mail* reported that the two sides were divided by three major issues: "what [LNG] price the potential buyers would pay; how much gas would be exported; and who would finance the $2.3-billion British Columbia pipeline and the liquefaction plant needed to complete the project" (Walkom, 1985 October 12, para. 2).

Second, the high infrastructure costs make it difficult for Canadian energy companies to launch the LNG sector alone; foreign capital's support is vital for the success of particular projects. This is a longstanding issue in all Canadian energy developments, especially the Alberta bitumen industry. Additionally, such support often involves the compromise of Canadian interests (e.g., adopting a minimal royalty strategy to attract foreign capital), which is unacceptable for many domestic stakeholders. This was a prominent issue during the public hearings for West Coast LNG. In November 1983, the NEB ruled that Canadian content was relevant to its final decision on the project (French, 1983 November 21). This decision was primarily in response to Canadian shipbuilders, vessel operators, and marine suppliers, who strongly opposed Dome's cost-saving measure of using the labor of Japanese contractors in LNG carriers.

Third, environmental concerns are at odds with extractivism, but their impact upon decision-making and public engagement around various projects differs substantively. In the news coverage about West Coast LNG, environmental complaints such as air pollution, marine ecosystem damage, and tanker safety were mentioned only peripherally. This suggests that in the 1980s, fossil fuel projects were predominantly framed as business matters when represented in the public sphere.

The cancellation of West Coast LNG forced Western Canadian gas producers to maintain their sole dependence on North American markets. In December 1996, the prospect of shipping LNG to Asia briefly resurfaced when a consortium of Canadian, South Korean, and US companies proposed Pac-Rim LNG, a $1.4-billion LNG plant near Kitimat in northwest BC (Boras, 1996 December 12). Targeting South Korea's growing LNG consumption, the proposal was endorsed by then-BC Premier Glen Clark, who expressed optimism following private talks with South Korean stakeholders (Authier, 1997 January 12). However, the project was short-lived: although an initial deal was reached in April 1997 ("Big LNG deal signed", 1997 April 17), it thereafter quickly collapsed as the 1997 Asian financial crisis spread to South Korea. Once again, an international market decline awoke British Columbia from its LNG dream.

During the first decade of the 21st century, a strong boom in primary commodity prices characterized the global economy during (Le Billon & Good, 2016; Veltmeyer & Bowles, 2014). Driven by strong industrial growth in China and other ascending economic powers, this boom led to record high prices for many primary commodities, starting with crude oil in 2001 and expanding to minerals and metals by 2003. This trend revived extractivism as a developmental path for many resource-based economies. In Latin America, it brought "re-primarization" and led a number of national governments to embrace the wave of resource-seeking foreign investment. This included Canada, where Stephen Harper and his federal Conservative Party, in collaboration with provincial conservatives in Alberta, sought to drastically expand the country's bitumen sector. Shortly after securing his first minority government in July 2006, Harper announced his party's vision to exploit "Canada's vast and seemingly limitless energy resources" (Taber, 2006 July 15, para. 3) and transform the country into a global "energy superpower".

As the Canadian economy embarked upon a renewed path of extractivism, reviving previously failed LNG development returned to the domestic gas industry's business agenda. In the early 2000s, however, major gas companies sought to make the case for importing LNG to North America in response to perceived shortages in domestic supplies. Before 2008 breakthroughs in shale gas extraction, the growth in gas production capacity stagnated in North America. Meanwhile, demand was increasing significantly, including the needs of bitumen production in Alberta and a surge in electricity and heating consumption during cold winter days, thereby pushing regional gas prices to new plateaus. Once eyeing Asian markets for selling their surplus stocks, Canadian fossil fuel advocates switched to the rhetoric of scarcity, predicting that ordinary consumers would be hit by a supply crisis if the region's tight gas inventories were not replenished by external sources.

In a 2003 report analyzing volatile gas prices, for instance, Canada's NEB chairman, Ken Vollman, warned that "consumers should expect no relief from whipsawing natural gas prices for at least three years" (Scott, 2003 May 6, para. 1) since Canadian producers no longer had spare reserves to meet growing consumption. Declaring the gas shortage a "brewing crisis", a *Globe and Mail* editorial (Den Tandt, 2003 June 10) went further by proposing that record-high gas prices "could stop the nascent U.S. economic recovery in its tracks" and even cause "Canadian consumers to reconsider the very notion of unlimited gas exports to the United States" (para. 3).

Driven by the panic over securing additional gas supplies, LNG resurfaced in Canadian energy discussions. Unlike its debut in the 1980s, discussions at this time centered on Canada's integration into the emerging global LNG market as an importer to serve both Canadian and US consumers. The key economic rationale was a noticeable price gap between imported LNG and gas from the Arctic. The cost of the former was expected to range between US $3 and $3.5 per MMBtu, whereas the latter would cost at least US $4 per MMBtu due to additional expenses from constructing the Alaska Pipeline project and the Mackenzie Valley project (Cattaneo, 2003 October 27). This difference convinced the gas industry that LNG imports would be a profitable business, fundamentally changing the dynamics of North America's gas markets, much like importing oil from the Middle East in the late 1960s and early 1970s.

With more companies joining the LNG frenzy, the number of LNG receiving-terminal proposals mushroomed in the United States and Canada. As of September 2004, there were 40 proposals under consideration or already announced, including two in BC (Morris, 2004 September 4). In May 2004, Calgary-based Galveston LNG announced that it would build an LNG receiving terminal near Kitimat, BC. One month later, another Calgary-based energy company, WestPac Terminals, proposed a similar project to be built at Prince Rupert, Kitimat's northwest neighbor. Given the similarity of the proposals, they entered a tight competition to attract investors, suppliers, and consumers (McCullough, 2004 July 26). Scheduled to begin operation in late 2008 and early 2009, both proposals came with an estimated cost of around $300 million and a daily processing capacity of 300 million cubic feet.

Galveston and WestPac pushed their applications through government reviews over the next three years (2005–2007). In June 2006, Galveston became the front-runner, receiving preliminary environmental approval from the province. Following this green light, it further confirmed potential buyers and pipeline construction details. Desperate to compete for investment, WestPac subsequently replaced the Prince Rupert proposal with a much larger project to be based at Texada Island, located in the Georgia Strait midway between Vancouver Island and the Lower Mainland (Mertl, 2007 July 31). With a price tag of $2 billion, the project included an import terminal and an associated gas-fired power plant. Cost increases also threatened the Kitimat LNG project (Hoekstra, 2009 August 7), including the construction of a $1.2 billion pipeline, Pacific Trail, to connect the terminal to the existing BC pipeline system.

As Galveston and WestPac promoted their proposals to residents at Kitimat and Prince Rupert, two narratives emerged in news coverage. The first one, which I call "vulnerable North", centered on the necessity of energy projects for job-starved rural BC communities. Echoing Harper's "energy superpower" rhetoric and the hype around Alberta bitumen, this narrative emphasized the employment opportunities associated with upcoming construction. It also implicitly legitimized resource extraction as the only viable developmental path for rural British Columbia. The sense of "no choice but resource-based economy" was captured well by the *Prince Rupert Daily News* after Galveston's project received its preliminary environmental approval. The newspaper celebrated the approval as a turning point in the Northern BC economy and predicted that "rising investment in natural gas, mining and related manufacturing, and transportation as well as housing and non-residential buildings are all leading to higher growth" (Vassallo, 2006 July 17, para. 2). Such boosterism for infrastructure investment was in part a function of business journalism reporting practices, but it also signified the enthusiasm for resource-driven development of many rural BC residents, a persistent trend that underscores ongoing urban–rural divides on issues such as fracking and shale gas exports.

The second narrative, which could be epitomized as "public fears over a potential explosion", centered on the environmental risks associated with LNG tanker traffic. Immediately following WestPac's announcement that it would relocate its project to Texada island with an additional gas-fired power plant, Gulf Island residents voiced concerns about the project's freshwater consumption, GHG emissions, and, most importantly, tanker traffic safety (Mertl, 2007 July 31; Vanderklippe, 2007 August 1).

> The Sunshine Coast and all of the Gulf Islands still have appeal for their ecological value, and to jeopardize that with the threat of tankers is not something that folks in British Columbia are going to accept very easily, if at all,

said Karen Campbell on behalf of the Pembina Institute (cited in Vanderklippe, 2007 August 1, para. 9). Environmental organizations, notably the David Suzuki Foundation and the Georgia Strait Alliance, expressed similar opinions. In 2008, the grassroots struggle against WestPac LNG consolidated into a social movement led by the Alliance to Stop LNG and Texada Action Now. By winning the majority support of Texada residents, the alliance forced the Powell River Regional District, Texada's governing body, to formally oppose WestPac's proposal (Webb, 2008 May 27).

The Texada controversy was similar to many other cases across North America during the same period. In St. Andrews, New Brunswick, local residents joined their Maine neighbors to fight plans for an LNG facility on the shores of Passamaquoddy Bay (Morris, 2005 August 22). In Quebec, communities around historic Quebec City rallied together in a strong pushback against the Rabaska LNG project on the St. Lawrence River (Stevenson & Perreaux, 2004 October 24). Public safety was the primary concern mobilizing such anti-LNG momentum. A few years later, this momentum was inherited by activists opposing the Christy Clark government's push for LNG exports.

Nevertheless, the frenzy over LNG imports quickly died down after 2008 due to the global economic downturn and, more importantly, the shale gas boom. As North American gas prices plummeted due to the explosive growth of fracked shale gas, industry was troubled by the fact that an excess of gas had turned it into a "wasted by-product" worth almost nothing (Prett, 2009 July 4). Desperate for potential buyers, Canadian gas producers once again turned their eyes to Asia. The Kitimat LNG project, for example, was transformed into an export project in September 2008 (Ebner, 2008 September 20). The Texada island proposal, on the other hand, quietly slipped into oblivion. The new cost of Kitimat LNG, including an LNG export terminal and the 463-kilometer Pacific Trail Pipeline, grew to more than $4 billion. Such an increase was far beyond Galveston's financial capacity. Eventually, in 2010, the project was sold to the Canadian subsidiaries of Apache Corporation and EOG Resources, two major fossil fuel corporations in North America.

3.4. Chapter Conclusion

The Canadian fossil fuel industry's push to revive LNG exports to Asia continued to make progress in 2011. In March of that year, Encana, another major corporation in the North American gas sector, joined the Kitimat proposal when it purchased a 30% stake in it from Apache and EOG (Healing, 2011 March 19). The shale gas boom in British Columbia also attracted the interest of transnational energy conglomerates. Shell announced in May 2011 that it would review the viability of building an LNG export terminal along the BC coast (Hamilton, 2011 May 28). One month later, Malaysia's state-owned Petronas, one of the world's largest LNG exporters, signed a $1.1 billion deal with Calgary-based Progress Energy Resources to collaborate on shale gas development in the BC interior (Cattaneo, 2011 June 3). As the world's largest LNG importer, Japan also joined the push for LNG exports in November 2011, when its largest fossil fuel corporation, Inpex, spent $700 million to form a partnership with Calgary-based Nexen.

Perhaps the most notable player amongst these transnational energy conglomerates was PetroChina, which expressed a strong willingness to invest in both gas extraction and potential LNG facilities. In February 2011, it captured the attention of many Canadian energy analysts by striking a $5.4 billion deal with Encana to form a joint venture, which, as argued by these analysts, demonstrated China's appetite for Canadian energy assets and strengthened investors' confidence in entering Asia's LNG markets (Jones, 2011 February 11; Vanderklippe et al., 2011 February 11; Yedlin, 2011 February 15). Although the Encana-PetroChina deal was later cancelled because the two sides could not reach a joint operating agreement, China's strong interest in BC LNG persisted. PetroChina, Korean Gas, and Mitsubishi (Japan) became the Asian partners of Shell's project. In October, Sinopec, another state-owned energy giant in China, made a $2.2 billion bid to acquire Calgary-based Daylight Energy (Vanderklippe, 2011 October 11). The acquisition was approved two months later, increasing China's access to energy resources in western Canada. As foreign investment flooded into the prolific gas basins in the BC interior, the governing BC Liberal Party began to position LNG exports to Asia as a generational opportunity pivotal to the future of the provincial economy.

To summarize, this chapter has presented an overview of fracking's profound impacts on the global LNG trade and British Columbia's natural gas sector. The historical review focuses on the pre-2012 period since it was largely absent from later news coverage on the BC Liberal government's LNG policies. Important contextual factors that shifted Canadian gas producers' perceptions of LNG since the 1980s have particularly been identified. The extended period of oversupply during the 1980s and 1990s led to early attempts at LNG exports. The failure of these attempts, however, did not prevent market dynamics from inspiring business interests in LNG imports during the early 2000s. A few years later, the shale gas boom brought energy investors' attention back to them.

Notwithstanding such directional changes, over the years, the North American gas sector has consistently promoted LNG projects using economic prosperity, employment growth, financial gain, and other individualistic discourses that echo the pioneer and frontier rhetoric embedded in Canada's staples economy (see Chapter 1). Occasionally, such an extractivist mindset is confronted by public criticism, as shown in the opposition movement participated in by Texada Island residents. Overall, though, LNG was not highly controversial in BC until the Christy Clark cabinet's aggressive promotion of it in late 2011. For now, this chapter concludes with three broad claims about the essential political economy contentions underlying British Columbia's quest for extractivist development.

First, BC LNG should not be defined as simply a "Canadian business"; it is fundamentally transnational, and its success hinges on favorable international market conditions and foreign investment. The collapse of the West Coast LNG proposal in the 1980s suggests that even with the joint efforts of several Canadian gas producers, building an expensive LNG terminal on the BC coast carries a high financial risk. Thus, in 2011, when the shale gas revolution revived the idea of exporting LNG to Asia, only transnational fossil fuel corporations joined the race. Nonetheless, even these energy conglomerates cannot fully bear the risks tied to volatile fluctuations in trans-Pacific LNG prices. Meanwhile, Canadian policymakers hold a shifting attitude towards foreign capital. Back in the 1980s, the provincial and federal governments acted mainly in a regulatory role. In recent years, however, they have increasingly acted as boosters for foreign capital's participation in Canadian extractivist projects.

Second, there is a persistent urban–rural divide in British Columbia influencing public perceptions of resource-based development. Rural communities have long suffered from a chronological economic decline due to the decrease in traditional resource industries such as forestry, fishing, and mining. Consequently, the fossil fuel industry has been left as the economic pillar of rural BC. Such a political and economic context has cultivated local residents' strong desire for infrastructure investment, which mobilized grassroots support for the BC Liberal Party's political campaign for LNG exports between late 2011 and mid-2017.

Finally, in terms of the environment, BC LNG carries risks associated with fracking as well as those associated with LNG terminals. The latter are unique to the BC coast's challenging navigation environment and have not been adequately explored in recent studies on the public opposition to shale gas extraction. As mentioned in Chapter 1, the protection of British Columbia's marine ecosystem became a common goal uniting anti-fracking activists and those fighting against bitumen pipeline expansion across BC.

References

Authier, P. (1997, January 12). BC premier hopeful of Korean gas deal. *The Calgary Herald*, p. A11.

Babaee, S., & Loughlin, D. H. (2018). Exploring the role of natural gas power plants with carbon capture and storage as a bridge to a low-carbon future. *Clean Technologies and Environmental Policy*, *20*(2), 379–391. https://doi.org/10.1007/s10098-017-1479-x

Big LNG Deal Signed. (1997, April 17). *The Vancouver Sun*, p. D6.

Bigl, B. (2017). Fracking in the German press: Securing energy supply on the eve of the 'Energiewende' – a quantitative framing-based analysis, *Environmental Communication*, *11*(2), 231–247. https://doi.org/10.1080/17524032.2016.1245207

Bomberg, E. (2017). Shale we drill? Discourse dynamics in UK fracking debates. *Journal of Environmental Policy & Planning*, *19*(1), 72–88. https://doi.org/10.1080/1523908X.2015.1053111

Boras, A. (1996, December 12). Calgary consortium plans $1.4 billion BC gas project. *The Vancouver Sun*, p. D4.

Bornemann, B. (2017). Private participation going public? Interpreting the nexus between design, frames, roles, and context of the fracking 'InfoDialog' in Germany. *Journal of Environmental Policy & Planning*, *19*(1), 89–108. https://doi.org/10.1080/1523908X.2016.1138401

Boudet, H., Clarke, C., Bugden, D., Maibach, E., Roser-Renouf, C., & Leiserowitz, A. (2014). "Fracking" controversy and communication: Using national survey data to understand public perceptions of hydraulic fracturing. *Energy Policy*, *65*, 57–67. https://doi.org/10.1016/j.enpol.2013.10.017

Brauers, H. (2022). Natural gas as a barrier to sustainability transitions? A systematic mapping of the risks and challenges. *Energy Research & Social Science*, *89*, article 102538. https://doi.org/10.1016/j.erss.2022.102538

Campbell, C. J. (2005). *The coming oil crisis*. Multi-Science Publishing.

Canadian content of LNG plan by Dome Pete may be only 60%. (1982, November 04). *The Globe and Mail*, p. B5

Cattaneo, C. (2003, October 27). LNG could be world's next big energy prize. *The National Post*, p. FP3.

Cattaneo, C. (2011, June 03) Time to vet oil and gas owners; Petronas deal for Progress assets part of trend. *The National Post*, p. FP1.

Den Tandt, M. (2003, June 10) Gas crisis could derail recovery. *The Globe and Mail*, p. B2.

Dodge, J., & Lee, J. (2017). Framing dynamics and political gridlock: The curious case of hydraulic fracturing in New York. *Journal of Environmental Policy & Planning, 19*(1), 14–34. https://doi.org/10.1080/1523908X.2015.1116378

Dodge, J., & Metze, T. (2017). Hydraulic fracturing as an interpretive policy problem: Lessons on energy controversies in Europe and the U.S.A. *Journal of Environmental Policy & Planning, 19*(1), 1–13, https://doi.org/10.1080/1523908X.2016.1277947

Ebner, D. (2008, September 20). Kitimat LNG switches plan to export, not import gas. *The Globe and Mail*, p. B9.

Evensen, D., & Brown-Steiner, B. (2018). Public perception of the relationship between climate change and unconventional gas development ('fracking') in the US. *Climate Policy, 18*(5), 556–567. https://doi.org/10.1080/14693062.2017.1389686

Evensen, D., & Stedman, R. (2017). Beliefs about impacts matter little for attitudes on shale gas development. *Energy Policy, 109*, 10–21. https://doi.org/10.1016/j.enpol.2017.06.053

Evensen, D., & Stedman, R. (2018). 'Fracking': Promoter and destroyer of 'the good life'. *Journal of Rural Studies, 59*, 142–152. https://doi.org/10.1016/j.jrurstud.2017.02.020

Fischer, F. (2003). *Reframing public policy: Discursive politics and deliberative practices*. Oxford University Press.

Fox, J. (Director). (2010). *Gasland* [Motion picture]. International WOW Company.

FracFocus. (n.d.). *What is fracturing fluid made of?* www.fracfocus.org/learn/what-is-fracturing-fluid-made-of

French, C. (1980, October 28). Japanese group agrees to buy LNG from Dome Pete. *The Globe and Mail*, p. B10.

French, C. (1983, November 21). NEB to hear Canadian-content proposal in LNG bid. *The Globe and Mail*, p. B9.

Gaede, J., & Rowlands, I. H. (2018). Visualizing social acceptance research: A bibliometric review of the social acceptance literature for energy technology and fuels. *Energy Research & Social Science, 40*, 142–158. https://doi.org/10.1016/j.erss.2017.12.006

Hamilton, G. (2011, May 28). Shell Canada says it's looking at BC coast for new LNG terminal. *The Vancouver Sun*, p. D1.

Harden-Donahue, A. (2011). *No fracking way: Our water, health and air at risk*. The Council of Canadians. www.canadians.org

Healey, S., & Jaccard, M. (2016). Abundant low-cost natural gas and deep GHG emissions reductions for the united states. *Energy Policy, 98*, 241–253. https://doi.org/10.1016/j.enpol.2016.08.026

Healing, D. (2011, March 19). Encana buys into Kitimat project; Pipeline deal will open LNG to Asian market. *The Calgary Herald*, p. C1.

Hmiel, B., Petrenko, V. V., Dyonisius, M. N., Buizert, C., Smith, A. M., Place, P. F., Harth, C., Beaudette, R., Hua, Q., Yang, B., Vimont, I., Michel, S. E., Severinghaus, J. P., Etheridge, D., Bromley, T., Schmitt, J., Faïn, X., Weiss, R. F., & Dlugokencky, E. (2020). Preindustrial 14CH4 indicates greater anthropogenic fossil CH4 emissions. *Nature (London), 578*(7795), 409–412. https://doi.org/10.1038/s41586-020-1991-8

Hoekstra, G. (2009, August 07). Oil, gas sector gives huge boost to economy. *Prince George Citizen*, p. 1.

Howarth, R. W. (2014). A bridge to nowhere: Methane emissions and the greenhouse gas footprint of natural gas. *Energy Science & Engineering, 2*(2), 47–60. https://doi.org/10.1002/ese3.35

Howarth, R. W., Ingraffea, A., & Engelder, T. (2011). Natural gas: Should fracking stop? *Nature, 477*(7354), 271–275. https://doi.org/10.1038/477271a

Howell, R. A. (2018). UK public beliefs about fracking and effects of knowledge on beliefs and support: A problem for shale gas policy. *Energy Policy, 113*, 721–730. https://doi.org/10.1016/j.enpol.2017.11.061

Intergovernmental Panel on Climate Change. (2022a). *Climate change 2022: Impacts, adaptation and vulnerability.* www.ipcc.ch/report/sixth-assessment-report-working-group-ii/

Intergovernmental Panel on Climate Change. (2022b). *Climate change 2022. Mitigation of climate change.* www.ipcc.ch/report/ar6/wg3/

International Gas Union. (2017). *2017 World LNG report.* www.igu.org/

Jaspal, R., & Nerlich, B. (2014). Fracking in the UK press: Threat dynamics in an unfolding debate. *Public Understanding of Science, 23*(3), 348–363. https://doi.org/10.1177/0963662513498835

Jones, J. (2011, February 11). Chinese shale deal could lead to more. *The National Post*, p. FP1.

Keranen, K. M., Weingarten, M., Abers, G. A., Bekins, B. A., & Ge, S. (2014). Sharp increase in central Oklahoma seismicity since 2008 induced by massive wastewater injection. *Science, 345*(6195), 448–451. https://doi.org/10.1126/science.1255802

Kevin, C. (1985, March 19). Consortium to try to salvage LNG deal with Japanese firms. *The Globe and Mail*, p. B3.

Klein, N. (2014). *This changes everything: Capitalism vs. the climate.* Simon & Schuster.

Kollmuss, A., & Agyeman, J. (2002). Mind the gap: Why do people act environmentally and what are the barriers to pro-environmental behavior? *Environmental Education Research, 8*(3), 239–260. https://doi.org/10.1080/13504620220145401

Le Billon, P., & Good, E. (2016). Responding to the commodity bust: Downturns, policies and poverty in extractive sector dependent countries. *The Extractive Industries and Society, 3*(1), 204–216. https://doi.org/10.1016/j.exis.2015.12.004

Lis, A., & Stankiewicz, P. (2017). Framing shale gas for policymaking in Poland. *Journal of Environmental Policy & Planning, 19*(1), 53–71. https://doi.org/10.1080/1523908X.2016.1143355

LNG Accord with Japanese Felt Uncertain. (1982, August 26). *The Globe and Mail*, p. B4.

Lush, P. (1984, October 31). Little gain seen in short-term energy export outlook. *The Globe and Mail*, p. B4.

Matthews, J., & Hansen, A. (2018). Fracturing debate? A review of research on media coverage of "fracking". *Frontiers in Communication, 3*, item 41. https://doi.org/10.3389/fcomm.2018.00041

Mazur, A. (2016). How did the fracking controversy emerge in the period 2010–2012? *Public Understanding of Science, 25*(2), 207–222. https://doi.org/10.1177/0963662514545311

Mazur, A. (2018). Birth and death(?) of the anti-fracking movement: Inferences from quantity of coverage theory. *Society, 55*(6), 531–539. https://doi.org/10.1007/s12115-0180305-3

McCullough, M. (2004, July 26). Ports vie to feed North America's natural gas habit. *The Vancouver Sun*, p. D3.

Medlock, K. B., Jaffe, A. M., & O'Sullivan, M. (2014). The global gas market, LNG exports and the shifting U.S. geopolitical presence. *Energy Strategy Reviews, 5*, 14–25. https://doi.org/10.1016/j.esr.2014.10.006

Mertl, S. (2007, July 31). $2-billion LNG import terminal, gas-fired power plant planned off BC coast. *Canadian Press NewsWire*. https://search.proquest.com

Metze, T. (2017). Fracking the debate: Frame shifts and boundary work in Dutch decision making on shale gas, Journal of *Environmental Policy & Planning, 19*(1), 3552. https://doi.org/10.1080/1523908X.2014.941462

Metze, T., & Dodge, J. (2016). Dynamic discourse coalitions on hydro-fracking in Europe and the United States. *Environmental Communication, 10*(3), 365–379, https://doi.org/10.1080/17524032.2015.1133437

Montgomery, C. T., & Smith, M. B. (2010). Hydraulic fracturing: History of an enduring technology. *Journal of Petroleum Technology, 62*(12), 26–40. https://doi.org/10.2118/1210-0026-JPT

Morris, C. (2004, September 04). Proposals for liquefied natural gas terminals are sprouting like mushrooms along the Canadian and U.S. east coast, but one in particular is fuelling opposition on both sides of the border. *Canadian Press NewsWire*. https://search.proquest.com

Morris, C. (2005, August 22). High-octane protest building in N.B. to proposed LNG facilities in Maine. *Canadian Press NewsWire*. https://search.proquest.com

Nikiforuk, A. (2015). *Slick water: Fracking and one insider's stand against the world's most powerful industry*. Greystone Books.

Olive, A., & Delshad, A. B. (2017). Fracking and framing: A comparative analysis of media coverage of hydraulic fracturing in Canadian and U.S. newspapers. *Environmental Communication, 11*(6), 784–799. https://doi.org/10.1080/17524032.2016.1275734

Prett, D. (2009, July 04). Swimming in natural gas. *The National Post*, p. FP9.

Scott, H. (2003, May 06). Say 'high' to natural gas prices: Analysts see little relief for three years. *The Calgary Herald*, p. D1.

Sigurdson, A. (1982, March 04). Govier report expected to increase BC gas estimate. *The Globe and Mail*, p. B7.

Sigurdson, A. (1982, March 08). British Columbia gas projects could mean new industry in the making. *The Globe and Mail*, p. R9.

Sigurdson, A. (1983, April 26). LNG prices to Japan declines. *The Globe and Mail*, p. B2.

Smil, V. (2015). *Natural gas: Fuel for the 21st century*. Wiley.

Smil, V. (2017). *Energy transitions: Global and national perspectives* (2nd ed.). Praeger.

Stephenson, E., Doukas, A., & Shaw, K. (2012). Greenwashing gas: Might a 'transition fuel' label legitimize carbon-intensive natural gas development? *Energy Policy, 46*, 452–459. https://doi.org/10.1016/j.enpol.2012.04.010

Stevenson, J., & Perreaux, L. (2004, October 24). Safety concerns may scuttle liquefied gas terminal near Quebec City. *Canadian Press NewsWire*. https://search.proquest.com

Stockman, L., Trout, K., & Blumenthal, B. (2019). *Burning the gas 'bridge fuel' myth: Why gas is not clean, cheap, or necessary*. Oil Change International. www.priceofoil.org

Taber, J. (2006, July 15). PM brands Canada an 'energy superpower'. *The Globe and Mail*. www.theglobeandmail.com/

Taylor, P. (1984, February 28). Dome Pete partner backs LNG project for one more year. *The Globe and Mail*, p. B19.

United States Environmental Protection Agency. (2022, June 09). *Importance of methane*. www.epa.gov/gmi/importance-methane

Vanderklippe, N. (2007, August 01). WestPac LNG plan may face backlash; Halts other BC project. *The National Post*, p. FP4.

Vanderklippe, N. (2011, October 11). China's new play for Canada's oil and gas. *The Globe and Mail*, p. A1.

Vanderklippe, N., Tait, C., & Hoffman, A. (2011, February 10). China pays $5.4 billion for BC gas play. *The Globe and Mail*, p. B1.

Vassallo, J. (2006, July 17). Northern economy finally turns corner. *Prince Rupert Daily News*, p. 1.

Veltmeyer, H., & Bowles, P. (2014). Extractivist resistance: The case of the Enbridge oil pipeline project in Northern British Columbia. *The Extractive Industries and Society*, *1*(1), 59–68.

Walkom, T. (1985, October 02). LNG deal with Japan expected to go ahead. *The Globe and Mail*, p. B9.

Webb, K. (2008, May 27). No power plant here, thanks; Texadans win backing to keep their island 'green'. *The Province*, p. A28.

Wolsink, M. (2018). Social acceptance revisited: Gaps, questionable trends. and an auspicious perspective. *Energy Research & Social Science*, *46*, 287–295. https://doi.org/10.1016/j.erss.2018.07.034

Wood, D. A. (2012). A review and outlook for the global LNG trade. *Journal of Natural Gas Science and Engineering*, *9*, 16–27. https://doi.org/10.1016/j.jngse.2012.05.002

Wüstenhagen, R., Wolsink, M. & Bürer, M. J. (2007). Social acceptance of renewable energy innovation: An introduction to the concept. *Energy Policy*, *35*(5), 26832691. https://doi.org/10.1016/j.enpol.2006.12.001

Wylie, S. A. (2018). *Fractivism: Corporate bodies and chemical bonds*. Duke University Press.

Yedlin, D. (2011, February 15). Encana deal sign of things to come. *The Calgary Herald*, p. D1.

Yu, C., Huang, S., Qin, P., & Chen, X. (2018). Local residents' risk perceptions in response to shale gas exploitation: Evidence from China. *Energy Policy*, *113*, 123–134. https://doi.org/10.1016/j.enpol.2017.10.004

4 Promoting BC LNG

Prosperity, Environmental Stewardship, and Global Competitiveness

Between late 2011 and early 2012, the British Columbia Liberal government led by Christy Clark published a series of policy documents and press releases (e.g., BC Ministry of Energy and Mines, 2012 February 03a, 2012 February 03b; BC Office of the Premier, 2011 October 26) that collectively announced an ambitious plan of establishing by 2020 a liquefied natural gas (LNG) sector targeting Asian markets. The plan subsequently developed into a high-profile controversy drawing attention from industry stakeholders, news media, and the public. The fossil fuel industry and its proponents applauded this move, echoing the government's assertion that the LNG industry will provide significant economic benefits to British Columbia and the rest of Canada. In contrast, environmentally conscious nongovernmental organizations, civil groups, Indigenous communities, and citizens expressed grave concerns over LNG's economic and environmental risks.

This chapter examines various pro-LNG public messages from late 2011 to mid-2017, when the Clark administration was in charge of the LNG development agenda. The empirical data in question consists of primary communication materials released by public and private stakeholders, such as press releases, research reports, blog posts, and opinion pieces. The analysis explicates how arguments and discursive frames embedded in these materials constituted a storyline of "progressive extractivism" by branding LNG as a bridge fuel with both economic and environmental benefits. Key to the storyline is the notion of a "once-in-a-generation opportunity": the extraction and export of shale gas promise employment growth for struggling rural BC communities, a path toward reconciliation with First Nations, and an unimpeded transition to a low-carbon society.

The storyline assisted the formation of a discourse coalition consisting of the BC Liberal government, the fossil fuel industry, and their supporters from late 2011 to mid-2014, during which the BC Liberal government's extractivist policies and rhetoric attracted as many as 20 LNG project proposals and helped the BC Liberal Party win a majority in the 2013 provincial election. As Asian LNG prices began to decline sharply after mid-2014, however, doubts and disputes emerged to divide the state–industry alliance, with some

DOI: 10.4324/9781003350620-4

industry stakeholders openly expressing their dissatisfaction with the Clark administration's hesitance to offer additional policy incentives for proposed LNG projects.

The sections that follow examine the major narratives of BC LNG proponents, thereby explicating the progressive extractivism storyline's strengths and weaknesses. Section 4.1 reviews prominent economically themed texts and demonstrates their framing of resource-based economic growth as the right choice for British Columbia's economic future. Section 4.2 discusses how falling Asian LNG prices from late 2014 to mid-2017 prompted prospective investors to withhold their support for BC LNG projects. Section 4.3 attends to the regulatory measures proposed for mitigating LNG-related environmental impacts. Building on consistent self-branding as a strong environmental steward, the BC Liberal government argued that the LNG sector under its administration would produce the "cleanest fossil fuel on earth" and generate "green jobs". Section 4.4 analyzes the "LNG or bust" mindset pervading resource-dependent communities across rural British Columbia, as exemplified by grassroots advocacy groups such as Fort St. John for LNG and the First Nations LNG Alliance. The chapter concludes with a critical assessment of the pro-LNG storyline's framing of shale gas development as essential for British Columbia's future economic growth and the provincial government as an extractivist state with responsibilities to facilitate, coordinate, and subsidize such development.

4.1. The Economic Opportunities of LNG

Extractivist economic development was the primary appeal employed by government narratives to legitimize pro-LNG policies. This appeal was deployed by defining economic struggles in rural BC communities as a policy problem and then LNG development as the ideal solution. Repeatedly highlighted in economically themed texts were references to potential investment, job growth, and tax revenues. "Over $20 billion in direct new investment, as many as 9,000 new construction jobs, about 800 long-term jobs, thousands of potential spin-off jobs, and over $1 billion a year in additional revenues to government" (BC Ministry of Energy and Mines, 2012 February 03a, p. 4) – these were the excessively optimistic figures the BC Premier office quoted in February 2012 when it announced the ambitious plan to have three LNG facilities in operation by 2020. Such bold estimates encouraged citizens, especially those living near potential LNG industrial sites, to image a major transformation of their economic prospects.

The mania over LNG's economic potential continued to grow in 2013. The February throne speech, for instance, dedicated an entire section to elaborating on forthcoming LNG revenues, aggressively campaigning over the projection that a "prosperity fund" supported by LNG revenues would reach a minimum of CAD $100 billion over 30 years, making the province debt-free by 2028 and even eliminating the provincial sales tax (Legislative Assembly of British Columbia, 2013 February 12). This sharp rise in policy attention to LNG – only three months before the 40th provincial election – sent a clear message to voters that the BC Liberal Party was determined to adopt it as a major pillar of their election platform. The section's depiction of British Columbia's abundant natural gas was classically neoliberal in its call for extractivist development:

> In BC, we are blessed with an abundance of natural gas . . . that can meet the real and pressing needs of other economies, especially those on our Pacific doorstep. . . . Seizing this opportunity requires that we add new value to this resource, converting it for transport to markets outside our continent for the first time. This can trigger a possible $1 trillion in cumulative GDP benefit to our province over the next 30 years. An estimated 39,000 new full-time jobs, on average, will be created during a 9-year construction period. Once all facilities reach full production, there could be over 75,000 new annual full-time jobs.
>
> (Legislative Assembly of British Columbia, 2013
> February 12, p. 8)

The section then noted that the economic benefits should not be taken for granted and urged BC citizens to rally behind the government to seize this "generational opportunity":

> Fellow British Columbians, this is the opportunity before us, but only if we seize it. It is not years away. It is now. Our province faces fierce competition from Australia and other natural gas producers. If we do not win the opportunity now, there may be no opportunity to win tomorrow.
>
> (pp. 10–11)

The source of the above hyperbolic speculations, however, was rarely publicized for scrutiny. Rich Coleman, the then BC Minister of Natural Gas Development, zealously defended LNG's economic potential in multiple interviews by claiming that the cited statistics and projects came from credible sources, including Ernst & Young Canada and KPMG (e.g., "British Columbia's LNG job claims disputed in new report," 2015 July 28). Yet, a closer examination of the reports (Ernst & Young Canada, 2014 February 18; Work BC, 2014 October 10) cited by Coleman reveals that the purported LNG prosperity is based on flawed assumptions. Their predictions relied primarily on government-given information and a highly idealized scenario in which Asian LNG prices did not fall below their 2012 average. The release of these reports followed the BC Liberal government's declaration in the BC Jobs Plan that LNG would be a robust job-creation sector (BC Office of the Premier, 2011 October 26). Given that no LNG-related economic analysis was published in the BC Legislative Library prior to the declaration, the oft-cited economic projections were likely based solely on internal government research. The lack of supporting evidence turned out to be a critical vulnerability of the pro-LNG storyline. Later in 2014, it was fully exposed by Asian LNG price decline, which enabled the anti-LNG discourse coalition to make compelling counter-narratives deeming BC LNG a reckless policy move filled with economic falsehoods (see Chapter 5).

Despite this vulnerability, references to LNG's economic potential dominated the BC Liberal Party's 2013 provincial election campaign messages, with then-Premier Christy Clark being the most outspoken advocate for the LNG "gold rush". Often appearing with a smile under a yellow hardhat, Clark's frequent visits to proposed LNG industrial sites were arguably her most memorable media images. Her LNG rhetoric integrated both government and party perspectives, a discursive construct commonly found in petro-states. Immediately after the 2013 throne speech, the Premier Office issued a press release claiming that

> the safe recovery and export of our abundant supply of natural gas presents an opportunity for prosperity unlike anything we have ever seen before. . . . British Columbians can secure tens of thousands of new jobs for decades to come by developing this clean energy resource and protect this new wealth for the benefit of all of us today, as well as our children and their families tomorrow.
>
> (as cited in Waterman, 2013 February 14, para. 3–6)

Echoing the Premier's pro-LNG rhetoric, a number of government ministries cited the anticipated substantial economic benefits to justify policy incentives for LNG development. In 2014, the Clark government introduced an LNG income tax framework addressing future LNG export revenues, and then-Minister of Finance Michael de Jong claimed that the framework would ensure revenues would be shared with British Columbians since it "strikes the right balance between a competitive economic environment and a fair return to British Columbians" (BC Ministry of Finance, 2014 October 21, para. 13).

Similarly, Shirley Bond, who led the Ministry of Jobs, Tourism and Skills Training, stated in her 2014 year-end review that "British Columbia has an unprecedented opportunity to create jobs and economic growth through the development of a LNG export industry; LNG will create jobs all over the province, thousands of new long-term professions for British Columbians" (BC Ministry of Jobs, Tourism and Skills Training, 2014 December 30, para. 5). Her ministry later organized a year-long, province-wide "Find Your Fit" tour showcasing tomorrow's in-demand occupations, which consistently presented LNG as an imminent sector that would drive future job growth (e.g., Ministry of Jobs, Tourism and Skills Training, 2015 October 13). While promoting the economic benefits frame, the tour also served as a coalition-building effort that sought to recruit and mobilize grassroots LNG supporters.

As the high initial costs of LNG terminals prevent them from being financed with domestic capital alone, the BC Liberal government targeted prospective foreign investors with a slightly modified gold rush narrative, branding British Columbia as an ideal destination for resource-based investment. Frequent trade missions led by Christy Clark or her key cabinet members exemplified this narrative. Fifteen of the twenty-four trade missions during 2014–2015 prioritized business discussions on LNG investment. As a further means of sustaining the momentum on LNG development, the BC Liberal government debuted an annual international LNG convention in 2013. According to the government press release (BC Office of the Premier & Ministry of Natural Gas Development, 2015 October 16), the 2015 convention attracted about 3,000 attendees and more than 300 exhibitors, which demonstrated promising interests in LNG from a wide range of stakeholders, including industry proponents and experts, investors, First Nations, market analysts, and prospective workers.

Nevertheless, the BC Liberal government's LNG outlook only received conditional support from industry stakeholders, who – while expressing interest in BC LNG exports to Asia – were not convinced by the optimistic predictions depicted in official narratives. In their view, the successful launch of the LNG sector hinged on whether the Clark administration could offer adequate policy incentives to mitigate potential business risks. Consider, for instance, the public communications of the BC LNG Alliance, the industry association representing major energy corporations behind proposed BC LNG projects. During the association's launch event in October 2014, its founding president David Keane reminded attendees (many of whom are members of the Vancouver Board of Trade) that:

> The new LNG industry in British Columbia is not a foregone conclusion. . . . If LNG is to be viable in this province, our industry, along with each level of government, will have to make some difficult decisions in order to cross the finish line. . . . We need to find the right balance that enables British Columbians to get fair value for their resource, while ensuring our industry can compete in world markets over the long term. . . . It's urgent we get this right as the window of opportunity to sell BC LNG into the global market is closing quickly.
>
> ("President of BC LNG Alliance says LNG not a
> foregone conclusion", 2014, para. 2–6)

In support of the industry stakeholders' requests for incentives, Canada's domestic fossil fuel advocates discussed the outlook of BC LNG from two perspectives. First, pro-industry think tanks embraced the fossil fuel industry's concern over profitability and advocated for additional tax and royalty incentives to reduce the infrastructure and operation costs of the LNG sector. The Vancouver-based Fraser Institute, in particular, stood on the media frontline and repeatedly warned the BC public about the necessity of launching the LNG sector quickly, with claims such as "Canada's window on LNG exports won't remain open forever" (Green, 2014 July 12) and "the annual [LNG] export revenues lost due to [regulatory] delay would be equal to between 2% and 9.5% of British Columbia's GDP in 2014" (Zycher & Green, 2015 November 17). The strategic exploitation of public anxiety underlying such claims epitomizes the collective push by fossil fuel advocates for additional government concessions to extractivism. The precarity of resource workers was also used to reinforce such anxiety. Referring to the Canadian Association of Petroleum Producers' influential "Canada's energy citizens" campaign (McCurdy, 2018), the Canadian Energy Research Institute (Simons, 2016 March 11) claimed that the prevalence of an anti-resource bias in BC public discourse had hurt families depending on resource jobs, and embracing the LNG opportunity was a recognition of Canada's hardworking resource workers.

Second, advocates of a Canada–Asia trading partnership endorsed LNG exports' economic implications by framing them as an opportunity to diversify Canada's international trade structure. In their view, British Columbia's growing ties with Asia would offset Canada's heavy reliance on the US market. The most prominent of such advocates was the Asian Pacific Foundation of Canada, which argued for years that British Columbia should serve as Canada's Asia–Pacific gateway by embracing LNG and other trade opportunities. For instance, the foundation's former president Yuen Pau Woo (2013 September 18) claimed that:

> The discovery of shale gas, and the subsequent race to develop viable projects, is the closest thing to a gold rush since the 1800s. It is also a game changer for North American energy trade and industrial development. . . . There can be no doubt about the enormous opportunity today to provide a relatively clean source of energy to buyers in Northeast Asia who are eagerly seeking secure long-term supplies.
>
> (para. 3–4)

Overall, discourses celebrating BC LNG's economic potential demonstrated many similarities with public controversies over shale gas in the United States and Europe, except for a twist: it was a reversed scenario, with the BC Liberal government begging the fossil fuel industry's participation in realizing the economic potential of BC-Asia LNG trade. As will be seen in the following section, the concerns of industry stakeholders regarding business risks and BC LNG's lack of competitiveness eventually led to a major dispute between them and the BC Liberal government.

4.2. The Ambivalence of Industry Stakeholders

Harvey (2007) argues that "competition – between individuals, between firms, between territorial entities (cities, regions, nations, regional groups) – is held to be a primary virtue" (p. 65) under neoliberalism. According to this doctrine, a neoliberal state is expected to pursue perpetual competitiveness through "re-regulatory" policies, such as the elimination of regulatory hurdles and the reduction of business operation costs, which enable private sectors to profit from performing state functions (Garland & Harper, 2012). As noted in the preceding section, the BC Liberal government and industry stakeholders disagreed on how to interpret the competitive edge of BC LNG.

The LNG blueprint, which initiated the pro-LNG discourse coalition, aimed to garner both private investment and public support. To achieve this goal, it highlighted political stability and responsible environmental steward-ship when addressing British Columbia's competitive advantages in the global LNG race. Accordingly, the province's major LNG advantages were listed as:

> (1) lower shipping costs, thanks to our proximity to Asia, (2) secure, stable government, (3) vast natural gas reserves, (4) high environmental stand-ards, (5) potential to access clean electricity, (6) positive relationships with First Nations peoples, (7) a well-established service sector, and (8) strong, updated regulations.
>
> (BC Ministry of Energy and Mines, 2012
> February 03a, p. 6)

The blueprint also elaborated advantages (4), (5), and (8) in relation to the BC Liberal Party's leadership in climate change mitigation. It claimed that, powered by clean hydroelectric power, BC LNG projects would fundamen-tally differ from competing projects elsewhere. Claims like this articulated a clear normative stance implying BC LNG's moral appeal in contrast to dirty fossil fuels.

Then, just prior to the 40th provincial election campaign, the BC Liberal government released a one-year update on the BC LNG blueprint, stating that the province was on track to have three LNG facilities by 2020 and that industry stakeholders had responded positively to its progressive approach to resource extraction (BC Ministry of Energy, Mines and Natural Gas, 2013 February 08). Statements like this reflects the party's concern that an aggres-sive pursuit of extractive policies could severely damage its progressive image among voters.

Skills training was another topic frequently featured in competitiveness-related official narratives. The BC Liberal government promised to re-engi-neer provincial education and training programs in preparation for the LNG sector's upcoming labor demand. As stated in *British Columbia's Skills for Jobs Blueprint* (Work BC, 2014 April 29), the planning for and training of

British Columbians would begin immediately to take full advantage of the LNG opportunity. The document listed a total of 15 recommendations; the most notable ones were recommendations #9 and #15, which promised government-funded apprentices to support LNG-related infrastructure projects and even permitted LNG developers to use temporary foreign workers if required by workforce needs.

The emphasis on a skilled workforce expressed the BC Liberal government's intent to create an investment-friendly environment by turning all its arms into promotional agencies for LNG development. By associating the LNG opportunity with skills training, the BC Liberal government also employed a "coalition confirmation" strategy (Metze & Dodge, 2016) to bridge the different economic interests of two different audiences: a business/corporate audience, to whom it tried to promote the LNG business case, and a public audience, to whom it boasted about LNG prosperity.

In short, the blueprint's portrayal of "progressive extractivism" centered on two issues: 1) downplaying the contradiction between shale gas extraction and its established environmental record, and 2) aligning stakeholder efforts to provide qualified employees for LNG facility construction and operation. Although, on the surface, the BC Liberal government acknowledged the importance of competitiveness, it was hesitant to cater to the industry's demands at all (political) costs. Consequently, its LNG policies were later trapped in the dilemma between neoliberal deregulation and political legitimacy, as shown throughout the creation of the BC LNG tax scheme.

The tax scheme that would be applied to LNG projects was a crucial element missing in the BC LNG blueprint and the subsequent one-year update. In October 2014, the BC Ministry of Finance (2014 October 21) formally released the province's LNG Income Tax scheme, setting the regular tax rate on LNG net income as 3.5%, effective from January 2017. The scheme included a special clause where, during the period when an LNG facility was initially constructed and operated at a loss, a reduced rate of 1.5% would apply until the payoff of all construction costs. Both rates would be locked for 30 years, and the LNG Income Tax rate would increase to 5% in 2037. To encourage investment, the tax scheme also included a new BC Corporate Income Tax Credit, which would reduce the provincial corporate income tax rate from 11% to as low as 8% for an LNG income taxpayer.

The release of the tax scheme was intended to sustain the momentum within the pro-LNG discourse coalition. In the official announcement, the BC Ministry of Finance (2014 October 21) claimed that the proposed scheme "is competitive with competing jurisdictions, including the United States and Australia", and the province's "advantage is more than just a competitive tax rate – proponents will benefit from British Columbia's skilled workforce, geographical proximity to markets and large natural gas reserves, as well as the cool, northern climate" (para. 8). Yet, the announcement downplayed a critical flaw in the government's economic opportunity rhetoric: the proposed rates were significantly lower than those initially promised, casting doubt on the economic benefits the LNG industry would bring to British Columbia. When the Clark administration released the scheme's draft version in February 2014, the regular rate was set at 7%. According to the BC Ministry of Finance, "the combination of declining LNG selling prices and increased construction costs" (para. 9) forced the government to settle on a lower rate to attract investors.

The tax reductions offered at the expense of the political credibility of the Clark administration failed to persuade industry stakeholders. As falling Asian LNG prices in late 2014 and subsequent years cast doubt on the economic viability of transpacific LNG trade, disputes gradually crippled the pro-LNG state–industry alliance. The BC Liberal government's reluctance to offer additional policy incentives to LNG projects came under direct attack from industry stakeholders and their advocates. They rejected the official stance that the existing incentives would be sufficient to compensate for market uncertainty. They also threatened to dismantle the pro-LNG state–industry alliance by denying final approval for proposed LNG projects.

For example, one month before the release of the LNG Income Tax scheme, Petronas claimed that it may pull out of its Pacific NorthWest (PNW) LNG proposal due to lack of appropriate incentives. According to Petronas's CEO, Shamsul Abbas, "rather than ensuring the development of the LNG industry through appropriate incentives and assurance of legal and fiscal stability, the Canadian landscape of LNG development is now one of uncertainty, delay and short vision" ("Petronas may pull out of BC LNG project", 2014 September 25, para. 3). Then in December 2014, despite receiving the province's preliminary environmental green light, Petronas decided to put its proposed LNG terminal on hold, citing high costs and unfavorable market conditions as the main reasons behind the decision ("Petronas puts BC LNG plant on hold", 2014 December 03). Petronas was not the only corporation worried about BC LNG's declining competitiveness. Around the same time, BG Group delayed its planned LNG terminal ("BG Group to delay planned BC LNG terminal", 2014 October 29), and Apache, which ignited British Columbia's LNG ambition by proposing the Kitimat LNG terminal, withdrew from the project and sold its stake to Woodside Petroleum, an Australian company ("Apache sells stake in Kitimat LNG project to Woodside Petroleum", 2014 December 15).

Notably, with difficult market conditions since the second half of 2014 threatening the economic viability of transpacific LNG trade, the BC Liberal government's pro-LNG messages encountered an unexpected group of critics: energy analysts and economists. Take US energy economist Kenneth Medlock as an example. Speaking at the Canadian Energy Research Institute's 2015 annual natural gas conference, he suggested that "we don't see any LNG exports from Canada until almost 2040" (cited in Johnson, 2015 March 03, para. 5), because (a) market changes made it barely profitable to ship LNG from North America to Asia, and (b) the high costs of building LNG plants from scratch put BC far behind the United States and Australia where existing LNG import facilities could be transformed for export at relatively low cost.

Whilst opponents of LNG development may interpret Medlock's prediction as proof that BC LNG had lost its economic ground, industry advocates reframed it as leverage to pressure both provincial and federal governments. Pro-industry policy institutes such as the Conference Board of Canada (Robins et al., 2016), the Canadian Energy Research Institute (Murillo, 2014), and the Fraser Institute (Green & Jackson, 2016) published reports warning that British Columbia could miss out on supplying LNG to Asia without immediate policy interventions. The policy recommendations they proposed centered on the neoliberal demand for deregulation. More crucially, these recommendations suggested industry stakeholders' intent to lead the pro-LNG discourse coalition by taking control of competitiveness-related discussions. Opinion pieces published in Canadian commercial media played a crucial role in amplifying fossil fuel advocates' voices (see Chapter 6). For example, the Fraser Institute claimed that "regulatory barriers and compliance costs" were responsible for LNG development delays:

> In January (2016), the federal government announced that it will require LNG terminal environmental reviews to consider both the direct and upstream greenhouse gas (GHG) emissions of these projects. . . . These new climate tests will only add to the regulatory barriers and compliance costs Canadian energy companies already face, compounding the effects that low energy prices already have on the industry. And non-development will also come with substantial economic costs. A recent Fraser Institute study found that the cost of delay imposed upon LNG investments in BC, defined as export revenues forgone, is substantial at C$22.5 billion per year in 2020, rising to C$24.8 billion per year in 2025.
>
> (Green & Jackson, 2016, para. 4–6)

The emphasis on high economic stakes in this excerpt served as a blackmail strategy to push for more government concession. The diagnosis on regulatory burden, however, contradicted additional policy incentives that federal and provincial governments subsequently added to the initial draft of the BC LNG Income Tax scheme. In February 2015, the federal Conservative government provided tax breaks which would "save the (LNG) industry about $50 million over the first five years" (Lang, 2015 February 20, para. 4). The Clark administration also allowed LNG investors to receive additional tax relief through its Infrastructure Royalty Credit Program (BC Ministry of Natural Gas Development, 2015 February 26). In response to Petronas's threat of cancellation, it further compromised by negotiating a long-term royalty agreement with the company, guaranteeing Petronas no tax or royalty increases for more than 20 years (BC Ministry of Natural Gas Development, 2015 May 20; Lee, 2015 July 14).

In sum, as the prospect of BC LNG suffered tough headwinds, discussions on competitiveness led to growing division within the pro-LNG discourse coalition. These discussions revealed how corporations' pursuit of profitability could conflict with governments' pursuit of public support, especially when changing market conditions exposed the fragile economic basis of extreme carbon projects.

4.3. The Cleanest Fossil Fuel on Earth

As discussed in my previous analysis (Chen & Gunster, 2016) of "LNG in British Columbia", the official information portal of BC LNG, a prominent discursive strategy of the BC Liberal government was the consistent branding of BC LNG as the "cleanest fossil fuel on earth", which attempted to legitimize shale gas development through environmental appeals. This discursive strategy was deployed primarily by symbolically contrasting the clean appearance of natural gas with the toxic and dirty appearance of bitumen from Alberta. In the collected data, two parallel arguments bolstered the notion of "clean LNG".

First, the BC Liberal government downplayed the environmental risks of fracking and liquefaction by defining them as a manageable technical problem only requiring minor regulatory adjustments. For example, when informing the public about fracking's environmental impacts, the "LNG in British Columbia" website stated that (a) the combination of safety measures and continuous oversight during fracking will offer sufficient protection of underground aquifers, and (b) water to be used by fracking operations will use only a fraction of BC's annual runoff.

Second, the BC Liberal government, in alliance with industry stakeholders and fossil fuel advocates, designated shale gas as a "bridge fuel" that provides an ideal near-term solution to climate change. Although natural gas has long been regarded as a better alternative to coal and petroleum (Smil, 2015), this feature became a prominent selling point only after the US shale gas revolution triggered widespread public attention to fracking (Mazur, 2016). As early as 2009, the American Petroleum Institute, the largest US trade association for the oil and natural gas industry, touted the idea that America's abundant natural gas would improve the nation's energy security and function as a bridge fuel to its energy future (van Ryan, 2009 November 9).

As for BC LNG, government actors responsible for environmental regulation and resource development were the primary voices delivering authoritative narratives highlighting this moral appeal. In her 2015 annual review, Mary Polak – the then BC Minister of Environment – explicitly referred LNG as BC's unique contribution to climate change mitigation:

> LNG will play a significant role in the global climate solution as countries look for a cleaner, transition fuel to replace dirty fossil fuels like coal and

gradually move towards 100% renewables. When nations choose LNG from British Columbia, they will do so knowing ours is produced in the most environmentally conscious way. No other LNG-producing jurisdiction on the planet meets our high standards. The export of BC LNG is truly both an economic and an environmental opportunity for the province.

(BC Ministry of Environment, 2015 December 18, para. 8)

Compared with the US context, the promotion of natural gas' environmental benefits had a slightly different start in BC. Back in 2008, the province became the first jurisdiction in North America to implement a comprehensive carbon tax under Gordon Campbell – Christy Clark's predecessor. This was undoubtedly a progressive move, but it was also based on political calculus in response to provincial voters' general consensus on environmental values. Given this legacy, the framing of LNG as a clean energy source by the Clark cabinet was driven by both political and economic motives. Accordingly, statements like Polak's sought to not only defend the BC Liberal Party's environmental stewardship among voters but also alleviate the concern over regulatory costs by deeming them as necessary for building the "clean LNG" brand. To a large extent, this discursive strategy resembles established green marketing rhetoric.

Among the Clark administration's press releases, texts referring to the "bridge fuel" designation typically boasted of the BC Liberal Party's strong environmental record. In 2014, the updated *British Columbia's Green Economy* document categorized jobs offered by the LNG sector as "green jobs" in a section titled "cleanest LNG":

Our [LNG] strategy is also founded on a commitment to maintain our leadership on climate action and clean energy. . . . LNG is changing global energy systems, and as a transition fuel it represents a real step towards a low-carbon economy. . . . China's decision to increase its use of natural gas from four per cent to eight per cent could eliminate 93 million tonnes of emissions each year – more than BC's total provincial emissions. It only makes sense for BC to want to be part of this positive global story, and we will do so in a way that maintains our environmental responsibilities.

(BC Ministry of Environment, 2014 March 14, p. 12)

This excerpt was also indicative of an appeal to administrative rationalism, which attributes the capacity to address environmental concerns to experts and elite bureaucrats, not to individual citizens (Dryzek, 2013). This theme played out consistently throughout the Clark cabinet's discourses on environmental risks, in which communities to be affected by fracking or the construction of LNG pipelines and export terminals were portrayed primarily as recipients of expert risk information. When outlining its efforts on public engagement and consultation, the Clark cabinet tended to frame growing public concern over fracking as arising largely from a lack of information and knowledge, which reinforced a technical–regulatory approach to risk management.

Echoing the BC Liberal government, industry stakeholders supported the argument that a low-carbon economy is more practical than a post-carbon economy. Natural gas, with its smaller carbon footprint than oil, presents a feasible low-carbon solution for the foreseeable future. In an information brochure titled "Natural Gas: Providing More and Cleaner Energy", Shell (2018) claimed that:

> Energy powers progress. Meeting increasing global demand while minimizing negative impacts on the planet and the air we breathe is one of the greatest challenges of the 21st century. A transformation of the global energy system is needed. . . . Natural gas will be a critical component of this energy transition – to generate electricity, provide heat for essential industrial processes, heat or cool homes, and transport people and goods over long distances.
>
> (p. 69)

For citizens looking for non-radical, gradual solutions to climate change, such a "pragmatic" approach to extractivism is undoubtedly appealing. Accordingly, BC LNG's civil supporters actively reproduced the BC Liberal government's talking points to undermine public concern over LNG's environmental impacts. Karen Ogen-Toews and David Keane, who frequently appeared in BC LNG news as opinion leaders representing Indigenous and non-Indigenous supporters for LNG development, wrote in the *Vancouver Sun*:

> British Columbia's LNG industry is being developed under some of the most-stringent environmental and regulatory oversight in the world. . . . Hydraulic fracturing has been used to access natural gas in BC safely and responsibly for more than 50 years. Every aspect of the process is regulated by the BC Oil and Gas Commission, including air quality and water use and disposal. The result is safe, responsibly developed natural gas that is delivered 24/7 to homes and businesses in more than 130 BC communities.
>
> (Ogen-Toews & Keane, 2017 May 8, para. 7)

That said, the alleged high environmental standards were meant to facilitate, rather than restrict, the extractivist agenda of LNG development. In August 2016 when the Clark government released a follow-up Climate Leadership Plan, it (BC Office of the Premier & BC Ministry of Environment, 2016 August 19) assured LNG proponents that "we are continuing to lead the way in reducing emissions and creating jobs . . . with an approach that balances environmental responsibility with economic opportunity" (para. 2).

This remark resonated with many fossil fuel proponents' conceptualization of regulation under a petro-state (Gunster & Saurette, 2014), with priority being given to resource-based economic development instead of environmental protection. Therefore, the gas-powered future society that the pro-LNG discourse coalition envisioned was compatible with the economic interests of the fossil fuel industry, with the fundamental goal of managing the process of decarbonization in ways that prevent radical disruptions to the global energy landscape, even though environmentally themed texts produced by the coalition acknowledged the need to address climate change.

4.4. LNG or Bust

Although the branding of British Columbia as an energy "promised land" that struck a balance between extractivism and environmental stewardship did not convince industry stakeholders, it was enthusiastically embraced by many rural BC communities for whom the promise of LNG investment represented not only a path toward economic revival but also a pragmatic solution to the tension between the fossil fuel industry and climate change. Many rural British Columbians constituted the popular base of the pro-LNG discourse coalition. In the collected data, their populist call for a rapid launch of LNG exports expressed two themes. The first drew on economic downfalls pervading rural British Columbia to urge government and industry collaboration to expedite the launch of the LNG industry. The second disputed the notion that BC Indigenous communities opposed resource-based development. Instead, some of them, with the Haisla First Nation near Kitimat being the primary example, threw their support behind the extractivist narrative that a partnership with corporations in pursuing resource-driven development could lead to hope and reconciliation.

"LNG or bust" – this binary narrative was the central message underlying both themes. By employing the rhetorical strategy of polarization (Dodge & Lee, 2017), it evoked a strong sense of desperation among many rural BC communities where resource extraction is widely viewed as indispensable for maintaining local employment. Take Fort St. John as an example. This industrial city in northeast British Columbia, located directly above the Montney Basin, has relied on the fossil fuel industry as its economic pillar for decades. In anticipation of a significant increase in hydraulic fracturing activities if LNG projects proceeded, the city adopted a pro-industry stance as soon as the BC LNG mania began in late 2011.

This stance had its historical precedents. Back in the 2000s, when drilling in the city's gas fields sharply declined due to high operational costs, it even pondered joining the neighboring province Alberta for more pro-industry subsidies (Harding & Cattaneo, 2007 July 5). When expectations for LNG exports stayed high in 2013 and 2014, Fort St. John experienced a mini boom, which was taken by the pro-LNG discourse coalition as evidence supporting the economic benefits frame. As the *Globe and Mail* reported, local residents were in an upbeat mood and forgot the doom and gloom they had experienced a decade before:

> While the BC government has been highlighting a flurry of proposals for LNG export terminals in the northwestern part of the province, the northeast is where the tale of the energy promised land begins. Signs of a mini boom are everywhere across the Fort St. John area. . . . Instead of doom and gloom, civic leaders are decidedly upbeat. . . . The region's airport is bursting at the seams; the local Walmart is starting a major expansion and the Winner's department store is preparing for a spring opening.
>
> (Jang, 2014 January 25, para. 14–17)

The story continued with a personal account from Richelle Cooper, a young college graduate who was on track to a fulfilling career in the natural gas sector. For Cooper, LNG offered the opportunity for a well-paid career, and her narrative was filled with optimism:

> Richelle Cooper . . . sees the energy industry as the economic catalyst for the region. A decade ago, there weren't nearly as many job opportunities for youth as there are today . . . she said after finishing a 12-hour shift as an administrator and labourer for Infinity Oilfield Services. "Natural gas development is creating jobs, and people are realizing that now", she says. . . . She already makes $22.50 an hour, but with some more training and experience, she is optimistic about landing a field job that pays $35 an hour and developing a fulfilling career.
>
> (para. 29–32)

Cooper's experience represented many youths in rural British Columbia who probably shared similar expectations for career opportunities. The upbeat forecast for LNG development thus incorporated grassroots political agency into a future-oriented extractivist discourse. Yet, as the LNG industry's rapid start-up faded away over the following months, frustration and anger replaced optimism. In February 2016, a public rally was held in Fort St. John, from which "Fort St. John for LNG", a pro-LNG citizen group, emerged onto the public stage. In an opinion piece written for the local newspaper, *Alaska Highway News*, the group's founder Alan Yu, himself laid off from the gas fields a month earlier, addressed natural gas extraction as the foundation of ordinary Fort St. John families' livelihoods:

> Let's face it: Fort St. John's economy is based on natural gas. We get food to our table directly or indirectly from natural gas operations. When there

is little activity in the natural gas industry, our economy takes a dive, and boy are we in a downturn these days. . . . What Fort St. John needs is a more stable and steady demand for our region's natural gas if we want to see sustainable economic prosperity. . . . This is why we need to support development of these LNG plants.

(Yu, 2016 February 25, para. 1–2)

His narrative then shifted to a blunt critique of vocal and "well-financed" environmentalists and a call for the "silent majority" in Fort St. John to stand up and grant social licence to LNG development.

The LNG "Forces of No" are very vocal about their opposition. They are well financed and well organized, and prey on the majority who are not well informed about the facts. This is why I started a positive social licence group here in Fort St. John called FSJ for LNG. The silent majority in Fort St. John must have their voices heard above these "Forces of No".

(para. 8)

Another noteworthy effort by Yu and his fellow LNG proponents was a road trip called "LNG or Bust". Between May and June 2016, they drove from Fort St. John to Ottawa to lobby the federal government to get BC LNG plants off the ground. The trip was crowdfunded, and on its GoFundMe page, Yu (2016 May 5) further laid out his belief that

the only way to lift our sagging economy is to increase the demand or market for our natural gas . . . and our advocacy for an LNG industry is getting resistance from foreign funded "environmentalists" even if economic needs and science is on our side.

(para. 3–5)

Yu's adoption of the "foreign funded environmentalist" rhetoric echoed conservative narratives found in the public contestations over Alberta's bitumen industry (Gunster & Saurette, 2014). At the heart of such discursive delegitimization was the conservative perception that environmental regulations and citizens who support them inhibit fossil fuel production.

As a public communication event, the "LNG or Bust" road trip only received modest attention from regional media (e.g., Fedigan, 2016 May 23; Scott, 2016 June 29), yet on its way to Ottawa, the team was joined by other unemployed oil and gas workers and participated in several pro-fossil fuel rallies (Yu, 2016 June 1). The trip also ended on a triumphant note with nine boxes of petition letters delivered to Bob Zimmer, the Conservative MP representing Northeast British Columbia. It is important not to overlook the road trip's communicative power at the grassroots level and the sincere desire it conveyed for LNG-related jobs.

The "LNG or Bust" narrative also resonated with some BC First Nations. Compared with Fort St. John for LNG, pro-LNG arguments from these Indigenous communities were formed around the idea of "resource extraction as a path toward reconciliation", which depoliticized Indigenous activism and reframed it in terms of further incorporation of First Nations into resource sectors. The primary voice amplifying this idea was the First Nations LNG Alliance, a collective formed in May 2015 by First Nations who had signed benefits agreements with the BC Liberal government and industry stakeholders (Hunter, 2015 May 26). As stated on the group's website (First Nations LNG Alliance, n.d.), its main purpose has been to "provide education and information to nations around our province [BC] as they consider economic and resource development opportunities when it concerns LNG projects in their territories" (para. 2).

Since its establishment, the First Nations LNG Alliance has been a vocal actor in the BC public sphere, frequently releasing statements, opinions, and reports that sought to bridge the "gap" between First Nations and the fossil fuel industry. It played a crucial role of re-articulating the pro-LNG coalition's interests in reconciliation jargons. In the aforementioned *Vancouver Sun* op-ed co-authored by the group's CEO, Karen Ogen-Toews, and BC LNG Alliance's CEO, David Keane, LNG was framed as a certain future for the BC economy, and "working together, First Nations and LNG companies are forging a new way of doing business in BC" (Ogen-Toews & Keane, 2017 May 08, para. 6).

Ogen-Toews further elaborated the "new way of doing business in British Columbia" in a series of blog posts focussing on "economic reconciliation in Canada". In her view, economic development should be prioritized to bring prosperity to Indigenous peoples. Collaborating with the state–industry alliance to launch the LNG sector thus offered the best option for BC First Nations to achieve the goals of reconciliation and decolonization:

> There are very many views of what reconciliation means. . . . In fact, I think reconciliation goals such as individual and community sustainability and wellness are linked to economic development and governance. . . . We see several setbacks every day to lofty goals of reconciliation – but, in my opinion the LNG Canada Final Investment Decision is a key indicator of progress on reconciliation.
>
> (Ogen-Toews, 2018 October 20, paras 1–3)

The call for "Indigenous partnership" by Ogen-Toews echoed efforts by government, industry, and think tanks to weaken Indigenous resistance in other environmental controversies preceding BC LNG (Neubauer, 2018). The very idea of "economic reconciliation" covertly conveyed the assumption that further incorporation of Indigenous lands into the capitalist system was the only solution for First Nations' sufferings. The conservative think tank McDonald Laurier Institute was on the forefront of media coverage promoting "reconciliation via resource extraction". Its managing director, Brian Lee Crowley (2016 October 28), for instance, wrote in the *Globe and Mail*:

> The news seems full of stories of what appears to be intractable Aboriginal opposition to such resource-based development. That may be, however, because the business community has not yet caught up to what the Indigenous world is trying to tell them. Look, for example, at the testimony of the First Nations Major Project Coalition with the support of the First Nations Financial Management Board (FNFMB) before a Senate committee this week. In the eloquent and elegant case laid out there by a Coalition representing 23 First Nations you can see first-hand what they are looking for to be willing and indeed enthusiastic partners in development.
>
> (para. 3–4)

Indigenous LNG proponents like the BC LNG Alliance only represented the minority views of BC First Nations. As Hunter (2015 May 26) noted in his *Globe and Mail* report, the majority of the 198 First Nations in BC chose to lean towards the anti-LNG coalition. For instance, the Lax Kw'alaams First Nation near Prince Rupert rejected a $1.1-billion offer from Petronas, which forced the energy conglomerate to revise its PNW LNG project (see Chapters 5 and 6). Grand Chief Stewart Phillip, then president of the Union of BC Indian Chiefs, also publicly raised concerns about LNG impacts on community health and living environments. Even within prominent examples of pro-LNG First Nations, the supportive stance of elected leaders has received continuous internal challenges. For example, Karen Ogen-Toews, the elected Chief of the Wet'suwet'en First Nation, clashed with the band's hereditary chiefs and eventually lost her position.

All that said, the arguments laid out by the First Nations LNG Alliance remain powerful, especially their call for prioritizing economic considerations in the reconciliation process. The most worrisome aspect of such a pro-industry stance is its ambiguous relationship with settler/colonial discourses offered by think thanks such as the Fraser Institute and the McDonald Laurier Institute. The ideas that "First Nations cared more about job security than political rights" and that "they were internally divided" symbolically undermine the political significance of Indigenous resistance. Moreover, as evidenced by the history of Alberta, "improved relations" between First Nations, the state, and the resource industries often result in the social legitimization of further extractivist activities on Indigenous lands.

4.5. Chapter Conclusion

This chapter has explored how the pro-LNG discourse coalition developed a versatile storyline to legitimize large-scale LNG development in British Columbia. The storyline frames shale gas as a morally acceptable fossil fuel, primarily by emphasizing its bridge fuel label and connecting it to British Columbia's strong environmental record. The branding of shale gas as a clean energy source was an attempt to divert public attention away from criticisms of LNG and downplay the urgency of decarbonization. The gold rush mentality served as the foundation for the plausibility of the progressive extractivism storyline, which facilitated the recruitment of grassroots supporters. The political agency of these supporters, however, was largely limited to partaking in an entrepreneurial framework set by the state–industry alliance.

Two flaws were evident in the pro-LNG messages produced by state, industry, and civic proponents: first, considering the negative social and environmental impacts of fracking (especially methane leakage), the clean energy label applied to LNG is especially problematic and misleading. Second, the higher production cost of shale gas compared to conventional natural gas renders its economic foundation fragile. As revealed by the pro-LNG coalition's internal division over the BC LNG tax scheme, it is difficult for extreme carbon to survive without various government subsidies. Taken together, employment opportunities to be created by the LNG sector are likely to be unsustainable from both economic and environmental perspectives. As the next chapter will discuss, both shortcomings were captured by LNG opponents for constructing the anti-LNG storyline. Shortly, this chapter concludes with three broad claims about the role of communication in the BC Liberal government's "progressive approach" to extractivist development.

First, the diversified discursive frames embedded in the pro-LNG storyline point to the growing sophistication and intertextuality of extractivist rhetoric, through which extreme carbon proponents coordinate symbolic resources to advocate particular economic and industrial practices. In the current case, the pervasive branding of shale gas as a bridge fuel builds on long-standing efforts by a variety of stakeholders, whose promotional strategies acquire much of their rhetorical force, ironically, from environmental discourses. The branding of shale gas as a bridge fuel hinges upon its contrast to the pervasive public perception of crude oil as dense, heavy, toxic, and dirty. In other words, the clean appearance of shale gas enables industry stakeholders to position it as a categorically different type of energy than crude oil. The urgency and magnitude of the climate crisis also create discursive space for promoting shale gas as an ideal alternative to other fossil fuels. Despite many environmentalists' (e.g., Klein, 2014; Suzuki, 2016 October 12) relentless efforts to explicate the absurdity of transforming our oil-based socioeconomic structure into a gas-based one, the commonsense semiotic connotations of "natural" and "gas" and the pragmatism embedded in "bridge fuel" narratives render this a relatively easy case to make, especially to citizens who are skeptical about radical climate change solutions.

Second, the progressive elements embedded in the Clark government's pursuit of resource-based economic growth expresses the BC Liberal Party's electoral calculations in recognition of the provincial political context as well as its willingness to act as an extractivist state on behalf of carbon capitalism. Although the Clark government did not, due to the fear of public backlash, offer total cooperation to foreign investors, the various compromises it made to boost BC LNG's competitiveness suggest the pervasive influence of extractivism in current Canadian economic policymaking. The LNG expansion is depicted as an unprecedented opportunity for everyone, but, essentially, its primary beneficiaries are transnational energy conglomerates profiting from the exploitation of nature. An extractivist economy could not bring marginal communities (especially First Nations) out of boom-and-bust cycles. When commodity prices collapse, these communities would be left with the devastating impacts of resource extraction.

Third, echoing Innis' (1956) analysis of Canada as a hinterland of other industrial economies instead of an independent economic entity in its own right, unconventional oil and gas have become Canada's new staples. It can be observed in the pro-LNG storyline how the dependency mindset has been reproduced in Asia–Canada relations, with Canada striving to become the supplier for emerging industrial powers in Asia. What have been intentionally neglected in the storyline are cautious reflections on whether British Columbia's booming economic ties with Asia offer any hope for changing the settler colonial nature of the Canadian economy.

In conclusion, the pro-LNG storyline presents an interesting twist on traditional extractivist rhetoric: it draws upon seemingly progressive talking points to justify resource extraction's continuing dominance in Canadian economic policymaking. How LNG opponents respond to such semiotic jujitsu will be discussed in the next chapter, which examines the counter-rhetoric of the anti-LNG discourse coalition, for whom the significance of resisting the LNG expansion far exceeds environmental concerns.

References

Apache Sells Stake in Kitimat LNG Project to Woodside Petroleum. (2014, December 15). www.cbc.ca/news

BC Ministry of Energy and Mines. (2012, February 03a). *Liquified natural gas: A strategy for British Columbia's newest industry.* https://vufind.llbc.leg.bc.ca/

BC Ministry of Energy and Mines. (2012, February 03b). *British Columbia's natural gas strategy: Fuelling BC's economy for the next decade and beyond.* https://vufind.llbc.leg.bc.ca/

BC Ministry of Energy, Mines and Natural Gas. (2013, February 08). *British Columbia's liquefied natural gas strategy: One-year update.* https://vufind.llbc.leg.bc.ca/

BC Ministry of Environment. (2014, March 14). *British Columbia's green economy: 2014 update.* https://vufind.llbc.leg.bc.ca/

BC Ministry of Environment. (2015, December 18). *World's cleanest LNG legislation comes into force.* https://news.gov.bc.ca/

BC Ministry of Finance. (2014, October 21). *LNG Income Tax ensures fair returns for British Columbians, certainty for industry.* https://news.gov.bc.ca/

BC Ministry of Jobs, Tourism and Skills Training. (2014, December 30). *2014 – a year in review.* https://news.gov.bc.ca/

BC Ministry of Jobs, Tourism and Skills Training. (2015, October 13). *Work British Columbia's find your fit to showcase British Columbia's in-demand jobs at LNG Conference.* https://news.gov.bc.ca/

BC Ministry of Natural Gas Development. (2015, February 26). *Unique program will attract investment, boost job creation.* https://news.gov.bc.ca

BC Ministry of Natural Gas Development. (2015, May 20). *LNG tax measures support balanced and stable tax revenues.* https://news.gov.bc.ca/

BC Office of the Premier. (2011, October 26). *Canada starts here: The BC jobs plan.* https://vufind.llbc.leg.bc.ca/

BC Office of the Premier, & Ministry of Environment. (2016, August 19). *British Columbia's climate leadership plan to cut emissions while growing the economy.* https://news.gov.bc.ca/

BC Office of the Premier, & Ministry of Natural Gas Development. (2015, October 16). *Third annual conference breaks new ground for LNG future.* https://news.gov.bc.ca/

BG Group to Delay Planned BC LNG Terminal. (2014, October 29). *CBC News.* www.cbc.ca/news

British Columbia's LNG Job Claims Disputed in New Report. (2015, July 28). *CBC News.* www.cbc.ca/news

Chen, S., & Gunster, S. (2016). "Ethereal carbon": legitimizing liquefied natural gas in British Columbia. *Environmental Communication, 10*(3), 305–321. https://doi.org/10.1080/17524032.2015.1133435

Crowley, B. L. (2016, October 28). The business case for reconciliation with first nations communities. *The Globe and Mail.* http://global.factiva.com

Dodge, J., & Lee, J. (2017). Framing dynamics and political gridlock: The curious case of hydraulic fracturing in New York. *Journal of Environmental Policy & Planning, 19*(1), 14–34. https://doi.org/10.1080/1523908X.2015.1116378

Dryzek, J. S. (2013). *The politics of the earth: Environmental discourses* (3rd ed.). Oxford University Press.

Ernst & Young Canada. (2014, February 18). *Analysis of the competitiveness of BC's proposed fiscal framework for LNG projects.* http:// www.llbc.leg.bc.ca

Fedigan, J. (2016, May 23). LNG or Bust hits the road to Ottawa. *Energetic City.* www.energeticcity.ca/

First Nations LNG Alliance. (n.d.). *About FNLNGA.* www.fnlngalliance.com/#about-fnlnga

Garland, C., & Harper, S. (2012). Did somebody say neoliberalism? On the uses and limitations of a critical concept in media and communication studies. *TripleC: Communication, Capitalism, and Critique, 10*(2), 413–424.

Green, K. P. (2014, July 12). *Canada's window on LNG exports won't remain open forever.* The Fraser Institute. www.fraserinstitute.org

Green, K. P., & Jackson, T. (2016, April 07). BC's snoozing while others realize our dream of LNG exports. *The Vancouver Sun*, p. A13.

Gunster, S., & Saurette, P. (2014). Storylines in the sands: News, narrative, and ideology in the Calgary Herald. *Canadian Journal of Communication, 39*(3), 333–359. https://doi.org/10.22230/cjc.2014v39n3a2830

Harding, J., & Cattaneo, C. (2007, July 5). Unnatural gas costs: Expensive drilling has fuelled a flight of cash and U.S. companies from Western Canada. *The National Post*, FP3.

Harvey, D. (2007). *A brief history of neoliberalism*. Oxford University Press.

Hunter, J. (2015, May 26). BC first nations chief creates alliance for LNG supporters amid backlash. *The Globe and Mail*. www.theglobeandmail.com

Innis, H. A. (1956). *The fur trade in Canada: An introduction to Canadian economic history*. University of Toronto Press.

Jang, B. (2014, January 25). BC's multibillion-dollar path to an energy powerhouse. *The Globe and Mail* (breaking news). http://global.factiva.com

Johnson, T. (2015, March 03). LNG exports from Canada a distant prospect, analyst says. *CBC News*. www.cbc.ca/news

Klein, N. (2014). *This changes everything: Capitalism vs. the climate*. Simon & Schuster.

Lang, A. (2015, February 20). LNG tax breaks will help, but is it too little, too late? *CBC News*. www.cbc.ca/news

Lee, M. (2015, July 14). Just how bad is British Columbia's LNG deal with Petronas? *The Tyee*. www.thetyee.ca

Legislative Assembly of British Columbia. (2013, February 12). *Speech from the throne, 39th parliament, 5th session*. www.leg.bc.ca

Mazur, A. (2016). How did the fracking controversy emerge in the period 2010–2012? *Public Understanding of Science, 25*(2), 207–222. https://doi.org/10.1177/0963662514545311

McCurdy, P. (2018). From the natural to the manmade environment: The shifting advertising practices of Canada's oil sands industry. *Canadian Journal of Communication, 43*(1), 33–52. https://doi.org/10.22230/cjc.2017v43n1a3315

Metze T., & Dodge, J. (2016). Dynamic discourse coalitions on hydro-fracking in Europe and the United States. *Environmental Communication, 10*(3), 365–379, https://doi.org/10.1080/17524032.2015.1133437

Murillo, C. A. (2014, September). *British Columbia (BC) Liquefied Natural Gas (LNG) economics*. www.ceri.ca

Neubauer, R. (2018). Moving beyond the petrostate: Northern gateway, extractivism, and the Canadian petrobloc. *Studies in Political Economy, 99*(3), 246–267. https://doi.org/10.1080/07078552.2018.1536369

Ogen-Toews, K. (2018, October 20). *Economic reconciliation in Canada: Part I, first nations participation in reconciliation*. www.fnlngalliance.com/blog/

Ogen-Toews, K., & Keane, D. (2017, May 8). LNG in BC – A certain future. *The Vancouver Sun*. www.vancouversun.com

Petronas May Pull Out of BC LNG Project. (2014, September 25). *CBC News*. www.cbc.ca/news

Petronas Puts BC LNG Plant on Hold. (2014, December 03). *CBC News*. www.cbc.ca/news

President of BC LNG Alliance Says LNG not a Foregone Conclusion. (2014). *BC LNG alliance news releases*. http://bclnga.ca

Robins, A., Owusu, P., Munro, D., & Coad, L. (2016). *A changing tide: British Columbia's emerging liquefied natural gas industry*. The Conference Board of Canada. www.conferenceboard.ca/

Scott, B. (2016, June 29). Cross-country LNG bus tour returns home with optimism. *Alaska Highway News*. www.alaskahighwaynews.ca/

Shell. (2018). *Natural gas: Providing more and cleaner energy*. shell.com/roleofnaturalgas

Simons, S. (2016, March 11). The case for LNG: Why our anti-resource bias is starting to hurt families. *Resource Works.* www.resourceworks.com/

Smil, V. (2015). *Natural gas: Fuel for the 21st century.* Wiley.

Suzuki, D. (2016, October 12). We can't dig our way out of the fossil fuels hole. *DeSmog Canada.* www.desmog.ca

van Ryan, J. (2009, November 2). *"Remarkable" natural gas.* American Petroleum Institute. www.api.org/

Yu, A. (2016, February 25). 'Forces of Yes' supporting natural gas and LNG must be heard. *Alaska Highway News.* www.alaskahighwaynews.ca/

Yu, A. (2016, May 5). *Campaign info page: Fort St.* John for LNG. www.gofundme.com/FSJforLNG

Yu, A. (2016, June 1). LNG mission to Ottawa an enlightening cross-country drive. *Alaska Highway News.* www.alaskahighwaynews.ca/

Waterman, J. (2013, February 14). Pathway to prosperity. *Alaska Highway News.* www.alaskahighwaynews.ca/pipeline-news-north/industry-news/pathway-to-prosperity-3473775

Woo, Y. P. (2013, September 18). *BC must be a 'gateway economy'.* Asia Pacific Foundation of Canada. www.asiapacific.ca/

Work BC. (2014, April 29). *Skills for jobs blueprint: Re-engineering education and training in BC.* https://vufind.llbc.leg.bc.ca/

Work BC. (2014, October 10). *British Columbia 2022 labour market outlook.* https://vufind.llbc.leg.bc.ca/

Zycher, B., & Green, K. P. (2015, November 17). *LNG exports from British Columbia: The cost of regulatory delay.* The Fraser Institute. www.fraserinstitute.org

5 Resisting BC LNG

Environmental Threat, Economic Sham, and Political Corruption

The aggressive pursuit of LNG development by the pro-LNG discourse coalition stalled between late 2014 and mid-2017 due to deteriorating market conditions and protracted negotiations between the BC Liberal government and industry stakeholders. Although the primary cause of this stalemate was the narrowing price gap between Asian and Canadian natural gas, LNG opponents' concerted efforts to reveal the multiple negative effects of LNG development were also crucial. Initially, these opponents focused on informing the BC public about the adverse impacts of increasing fracking activities. Over time, however, the pro-LNG discourse coalition's narratives opened a number of additional areas of criticism, notably the threat of fossil fuel lobbying to democratic governance, Canada's relentless infringement of Indigenous rights, and the fragile economic basis of BC LNG exports to Asia.

As an increasing number of citizens began to question the promises made by the progressive extractivism storyline, the BC Liberal Party's popularity was in jeopardy. A 2016 survey conducted by pollster Insight West found considerable animosity towards fracking and LNG exports (Hoekstra, 2016 March 23). Among the over 800 survey participants, 41% opposed the BC Liberal government's aggressive pursuit of LNG, and 61% expressed concern about the increase of fracking activities. Compared to a similar poll conducted in 2013, both results increased by more than 10%. Then one year later, the BC Liberal Party failed to secure a majority government in the 41st provincial election. The slow progress of the promised LNG development was recognized as a major contributing factor to this outcome (Rankin & McElroy, 2017 April 11), providing indirect evidence of the anti-LNG discourse coalition's public influence.

This chapter analyzes how LNG opponents, who formed an anti-LNG discourse coalition, employed various discursive frames to transform the anti-LNG storyline from conventional environmental advocacy to broader public discussions on British Columbia's political economy. The storyline not only rejected LNG development as the only viable option for reviving rural communities but also provided extensive discussions on policy alternatives and their potential to steer the province away from extractivism. The diverse

DOI: 10.4324/9781003350620-5

membership of the anti-LNG discourse coalition included progressive advocacy groups, environmental organizations, concerned citizens, and Indigenous
activists. The progressive think tank Canadian Centre for Policy Alternatives
(CCPA), the independent media Tyee, and the online blog Common Sense
Canadians have provided the essential digital discursive space for opponents
of LNG to communicate with one another and with the general public.

5.1. The Inconvenient Truth of LNG's Environmental Impacts

As discussed in the previous chapter, the BC Liberal government constructed
the "clean LNG" frame to distract public attention from LNG's environmental risks. For example, the "LNG in British Columbia" website depicted the
LNG industry's daily operations as four straightforward steps: first, shale gas
is extracted via hydraulic fracturing; then it is transported via pipelines to
coastal liquefaction plants; next, these plants transform shale gas into LNG;
finally, LNG is loaded onto specially designed tankers and shipped to Asian
markets. In the view of the anti-LNG discourse coalition, this simplification
grossly misrepresented the significant social and environmental costs associated with the production, transportation, liquefaction, and exportation of shale
gas. To deconstruct the "clean LNG" frame, coalition members issued a series
of environmental risk and degradation-focused warnings to the BC public.
This "environmental risk" frame dominated anti-LNG communications during the initial phase of the BC LNG controversy.

In contrast to government and industry stakeholders who adopted the technical expressions "hydraulic fracturing" or "shale extraction", LNG opponents
overwhelmingly labeled the production process as "fracking" – a colloquial term
with harsh and destructive connotations. Initially popularized in public awareness by *Gasland* (Fox, 2010), the term has become associated with the horrifying "lighting water on fire" image, which speaks to fracking's serious threat to
contaminate water supplies. In the current case, the anti-LNG discourse coalition's deliberate choice of the term drew on widespread public distrust, which
symbolically linked British Columbia's pursuit of becoming an LNG-exporting
juggernaut to a global trend, with booming unconventional fossil fuel production
threatening many communities' public health and living environment. According to David Suzuki (2015 January 06), Canada's best-known environmentalist,

> LNG should be labelled liquefied fracked gas (LFG): it requires pump-
> ing millions of litres of chemical-laced water deep underground to shatter
> shale and liberate embedded gas; and it is a short-term way to get energy
> with long-term ecological impacts on water and whatever organisms might
> be down there.
>
> (para. 9)

The anti-LNG discourse coalition considered an immediate nationwide ban on fracking as essential to safeguard the local environment and avert a looming global crisis caused by the increased extraction and consumption of unconventional fossil fuels. In November 2017, a consortium of 17 organizations consisting of prominent environmental and Indigenous groups (e.g., the David Suzuki Foundation, the Sierra Club of BC, the Union of BC Indian Chiefs, etc.) demanded a full public inquiry into fracking operations. Such an inquiry, the consortium insisted, was a necessary step given "escalating water usage by fracking companies, their poor or misleading consultations with First Nations, widespread industry non-compliance with relevant provincial water laws through the construction of dozens of unlicensed dams, and record-setting induced earthquakes at BC fracking operations" (Sierra Club BC, 2017, para. 3). The broader anti-LNG storyline later incorporated this anti-fracking sentiment.

Among the various fracking-related concerns raised by activists, two were of particular importance: how fracking would irreversibly damage British Columbia's natural wealth, threatening its water safety in particular, and the widespread belief that natural gas is a clean energy resource. The abundant water resources of British Columbia are essential for sustaining regional ecological systems and rural communities; consequently, the prospect of dramatic increases in industrial water usage associated with fracking alarmed a great number of rural residents. The use of chemicals during fracking operations has also sparked widespread concern for the safety of drinking water.

Aware of the public's environmental concerns, the BC Liberal government took proactive measures to defend fracking. For example, the "LNG in British Columbia" website claimed that (1) the combination of safety measures and continuous oversight during fracking will offer sufficient protection of underground aquifers, and (2) water to be used by fracking operations will use only a very small percentage of British Columbia's annual runoff. To refute such claims, the anti-LNG coalition argued in a series of interconnected public messages that the BC Liberal government deliberately understated the number of new wells that would need to be drilled and that the amount of water consumed by these wells would far exceed official estimates. According to CCPA's estimation, to meet only 70% of the capacity of British Columbia's proposed LNG plants, "roughly 39,000 new wells would be required by 2040, and . . . a very conservatively estimated 582 billion litres of water would then be polluted and removed from the hydrological cycle" (Parfitt & Hughes, 2014, para. 9). Moreover, as the water used in fracking becomes toxic and irrecoverable, fracking causes further damage to the regional hydrological cycle in British Columbia.

Natural gas is considered a cleaner alternative to other fossil fuels due to the fact that its combustion produces fewer greenhouse gas (GHG) emissions. This was the basis of the pro-LNG discourse coalition's relentless promotion of the environmental benefits of shale gas. In response, LNG opponents sought to debunk the widespread perception of shale gas as a clean fossil fuel by underlining LNG's hidden climate costs. Central to their discussions of LNG's environmental impact were two arguments. First, constant methane leakage from fracked wells, known as fugitive emissions, offsets shale gas's environmental advantage against other fossil fuels. As a potent GHG, methane has a much higher warming potential than CO_2 over a 20-year period (Lee, 2012). The problem of fugitive emissions is made even worse by flaring, a common practice during gas production. As noted by *DeSmog Canada*, "methane emissions from British Columbia's natural gas industry are likely at least seven times greater than official numbers blowing British Columbia's Climate Action Plan out of the water" (Leahy, 2013 May 8, para. 2). Second, increasing the supply of gas to Asia does not necessarily lead to the displacement of coal-fired electricity plants there (Leahy, 2013 March 14). Without strong climate policies, such additional supply simply feeds the current model of carbon-intensive economic growth.

Within the anti-LNG coalition, progressive think tanks such as CCPA and the Pembina Institute played a leading role in publishing studies explicating BC LNG's implications for climate change. For example, in a report titled *LNG and climate change: the global context*, Matt Horne and Josha MacNab (2014) from the Pembina Institute made the case that whether LNG could weed out coal is not a market-driven issue, and natural gas's role as a bridge fuel makes sense only if it is quickly phased out around 2030. Considering all factors, the proposed BC LNG expansion is by no means a climate solution. Many LNG opponents expressed the concern that British Columbia's LNG ambition would lock itself into dependency on the fossil fuel industry, thereby slowing the transition to a truly sustainable economy. To strengthen this criticism, LNG opponents used various metaphors to highlight the hypocrisy embedded in British Columbia's climate politics: LNG was presented as a "carbon bomb" (Lee, 2012), a "dirty secret on the west coast" (McCartney, 2016), and a "fraud" filled with broken promises (Nikiforuk, 2016 November 10). An example of the critique of fossil fuel lock-in was offered by Seth Klein (2015 December 28) from the CCPA:

> While the Alberta Tar Sands may represent Canada's largest source of greenhouse gases, were BC to succeed in realizing its LNG dream, this new industry (along with the fracking fields in British Columbia's North East needed to fuel it) would constitute Canada's next largest "carbon bomb".... It makes no sense to encourage and facilitate the investment of billions of dollars in new long-term fossil fuel infrastructure when the logic of the Paris agreement tells us we should be managing our natural gas industry for wind-down, not ramp up.
>
> (para. 7–9)

Another key selling point used by the BC Liberal government in its green branding of LNG concerned the electricity used during liquefying shale gas. The original BC LNG blueprint (BC Ministry of Energy and Mines, 2012 February 03) claimed that "LNG development in BC will have lower life cycle greenhouse gas emissions than anywhere else in the world by promoting the use of clean electricity to power LNG plants" (p. 7). This assertion was based on the widely available hydropower in the province, with 95% of its electricity coming from hydroelectric generating stations. Considering the significant increase in electricity demanded by LNG plants, however, where additional capacity would come from became a challenging issue.

The BC LNG blueprint left the question unanswered, but activists soon found the hidden connection between the LNG sector and Site C, a mega dam project surrounded by decades-long controversies (Eagle, 2017 March 23). In December 2014, the BC Liberal government rushed to a controversial approval of Site C. As the construction of Site C accelerated amid protests and legal challenges, independent media began to investigate scandals surrounding the approval process. Reports from *DeSmog Canada*, the *Tyee*, and *National Observer* (e.g., Ball, 2014 December 16; Bell, 2017 August 09; Gilchrist, 2015 June 12; Lavoie, 2014 May 27; Parfitt, 2016 February 4) explicated how LNG played a decisive role in Site C's controversial approval.

These discursive efforts forged an alliance between anti-Site C and anti-LNG activists, who collectively challenged Site C on economic, democratic, and environmental grounds. The opposition concentrated on nearly 4,000 hectares of farmland across the Peace River Valley that would be flooded for dam construction. The issue of using clean energy to power dirty fossil fuel production was also discussed extensively. For example, both David Suzuki and Grand Chief Stewart Phillip (head of the Union of BC Indian Chiefs) condemned Site C as a climate change disaster (Prystupa, 2016 February 23). In another critical report published in the *National Observer*, Warren Bell (2017 August 09) defined Site C as a 21st-century Titanic and unmasked the absurdity embedded in the LNG–Site C linkage:

Using so-called "clean energy" to supply power to one of the "dirtiest" sources of energy may seem like a public relations coup, but in this case, it's actually more like double trouble – the kind of tactic only a climate change-denying, fossil fuel industry-besotted government would resort to. For starters, hydroelectric energy isn't all that clean, because large amounts of methane gas are produced by decaying vegetation flooded upstream from dams. For another, the reputation that natural gas itself has earned as a "clean" fossil fuel – to be used as a "bridge" fuel between coal and oil and renewable energy – has been robustly challenged. Some independent researchers have amassed strong evidence that fracking causes greater global warming effects than the fossil fuel usually condemned as the dirtiest of all: coal.

(para. 47–48)

In conclusion, the anti-LNG discourse coalition, drawing upon the profound and enduring influence of environmentalism in British Columbia, infused its criticism with specific information regarding the global and local environmental impacts of the LNG industry. Despite being well perceived among urban BC residents, the communication of environmental threats was unable to overcome the "LNG or bust" rhetoric prevalent in rural BC communities. Recognizing this challenge, the anti-LNG coalition went beyond the traditional "jobs versus the environment" dichotomy by attending to the economic prospect of transpacific LNG trade.

5.2. Questioning LNG's Economic Outlook

Media and policy discourses typically characterize fracking as either an economic opportunity or an environmental threat. This "jobs versus the environment" dichotomy has emerged as a principal contention in recent fracking controversies, bolstered by discursive struggles between antagonistic stakeholders (Dodge & Metze, 2017; Matthews & Hansen, 2018; Olive & Delshad, 2017). However, the public debates regarding BC LNG did not simply replicate the dichotomy.

Informed by the contradiction between LNG proponents' claims and analysts' economic forecasts (see Chapter 4), LNG opponents identified BC LNG's market sensitivity as a glaring weakness of the pro-LNG storyline. Accordingly, they engaged actively with business analyses of BC LNG's economic prospects. Critical interpretations of global LNG market trends thus played a unique and significant role in anti-LNG narratives. With the post-2014 decline in Asian LNG prices fully exposing market volatility, opponents exerted considerable effort to undermine BC LNG's economic appeal. They characterized the reckless pursuit of transpacific LNG trade as a high-risk venture with a low return on public investment. The critical discussions on extractivism's economic appeal offered an alternative vision of prosperity and echoed public concern regarding fracking's environmental impacts. CCPA and its affiliated "Policy Note" website were the most prominent proponents of this "economic uncertainty" frame. Consequently, the analysis that follows focuses primarily on CCPA publications.

The economic uncertainty frame was developed after the BC Liberal government dramatically boosted its prediction of LNG's economic potential in its 2013 *Speech from the Throne*. Prior to the speech, the CCPA's critiques of LNG, like those of many other LNG opponents, focused on environmental concerns regarding fracking. In late 2011, the CCPA published a policy brief titled *Fracking Up Our Water, Hydro Power, and Climate* (Parfitt, 2011 November 9) shortly after LNG export was identified as an economic pillar in the *BC Jobs Plan*. Weighing LNG's projected economic benefits against the significant environmental costs, this brief defined the pursuit of shale gas developments as a reckless policy move, making no sense for either climate or economy. It suggested that instead of subsidizing a polluting industry, the BC Liberal government should work to increase employment in green sectors.

The contradiction between economic growth and environmental protection remained a major theme in subsequent CCPA publications. Nonetheless, as shifting market dynamics in Asia clouded BC LNG's economic outlook, discussions on it gradually gave way to an economic narrative in which CCPA incorporated numerous arguments and statistics from energy analysts to draw public attention to the economic risks of transpacific LNG trade. Exemplifying this shift in discursive strategy was a policy brief series called "LNG Reality Check".

In April 2014, CCPA released the series' first report, titled *Path to Prosperity* (Lee, 2014 April), which took issue with the provincial government's promise of a $100 billion Prosperity Fund arising from LNG revenues over 30 years. By digging into government statistics and estimates released by energy market analysts, the report asserted that substantial new LNG supplies coming onto world markets would enable Asian importers to press for lower prices. It also argued that implementing the LNG income tax at 7% – the necessary rate to generate the promised revenues – would be unrealistic with the growing downward pressure and the massive capital investment required to establish LNG export from scratch. Consequently, the report framed the Prosperity Fund as a proposal filled with empty promises because its primary revenue source was likely to diminish following LNG's changing global supply-and-demand conditions:

> If BC received top ($16) prices and sold 82 Mt of LNG, oil and gas companies would make over $600 billion in total profits. In this best-of-all-possible-worlds scenario . . . BC could meet its revenue target of $100 billion over 30 years (including corporate income tax). However, global supply and demand conditions for LNG suggest a lowering of expectations about both the price BC is likely to receive in Asia and the quantities that will be exported. For low to medium production levels at a $14 price in Asia, these revenues would range from $20 to $48 billion over 30 years; at a $12 price, $12 to $29 billion over 30 years (including corporate income tax).
>
> (Lee, 2014, p. 13)

One year later, *A Clear Look at BC LNG* (Hughes, 2015) updated the analysis of LNG's projected contribution to British Columbia's economy. At that time, as Asian LNG prices were already caught in a downward trend, the update not only reiterated the considerable economic risks associated with LNG development but also directly discredited industry-friendly think tanks' overtly positive estimates. When challenging the Canadian Energy Research Institute's estimates, the update's author, David Hughes, an ex-industry expert with knowledge about energy investment, argued that the economic basis of BC LNG had already disappeared:

> The cost of liquefaction, transport and regasification in moving LNG to China or Japan from Canada's west coast is estimated by the Canadian Energy Research Institute (CERI) as U.S. $4.50 to $7.00 per million BTUs (MMBtu). . . . Assuming an average cost of $6.00 to move the gas and a domestic gas price of $4.00, market conditions have already eliminated the arbitrage, as landed LNG prices in Japan and Korea were estimated at $7.45 per MMBtu in June 2015 and $7.30 in China. China has also recently secured long-term gas supply commitments via pipeline from Russia, which will dampen upward movement in LNG prices there. The recent drop in oil prices may also affect the profitability of oil-linked LNG contracts, especially if it continues in the longer term.
>
> (Hughes, 2015, p. 44)

To further alter the BC public's blind optimism about LNG development's job-creation potential, CCPA elaborated its concern over economic uncertainties with a point-by-point rebuttal of relevant official claims (Lee, 2015a). It pointed out that Grant Thornton, the consultancy commissioned to develop employment estimates, made its analysis based on information provided by the BC Liberal government. Accordingly, "there was no practical reason for Grant Thornton to be hired to use the government's own numbers and model apart from providing the appearance of independent justification for an absurdly large jobs number" (Lee, 2015a, p. 4). Research into the "100,000 jobs" number found that almost every step in Grant Thornton's estimation process was overly optimistic. By comparison, CCPA's independent calculation indicated that even if BC were able to achieve a modest beginning of LNG export, its actual job-creation capacity would be limited to "only 2,000 to 3,000 construction jobs per plant over three years and 200 to 300 permanent workers once operational" (Lee, 2015a, p. 1). Furthermore, some of these jobs could be taken by "fly-in, fly-out" workers instead of local ones.

The strategic engagement with mainstream economic analyses by CCPA demonstrates a unique approach to altering public perceptions of resource development. Not only did the discussions of BC LNG's dubious business model shake the economic foundation of pro-LNG narratives, but they also enabled opponents to confront the BC Liberal Party's political motives and assert that its extractivist policies betray the public interest. In his summary of the "LNG Reality Check" series' major findings, Marc Lee, CCPA's Senior Economist, warned the BC public that there was "a pattern of misinformation about LNG – coming primarily from the BC Liberal government, which should be looking out for the public interest instead of blindly championing the industry" (Lee, 2015c November 12, para. 1).

Other members of the anti-LNG discourse coalition embraced CCPA's critical questioning of BC LNG's abysmal economics. Besides plunging Asian LNG prices, their economic discussions further highlighted the following issues: (1) the construction of Site C would add a heavy burden to the provincial budget and force ordinary households to pay the electricity cost of liquefaction (Shaffer, 2016); (2) the BC Liberal government's desperation to launch the LNG industry resulted in substantial concessions to industry stakeholders, which dragged taxpayers into a gamble with slim odds and puny returns (Nikiforuk, 2016 November 10); and (3) instead of subsidizing the fossil fuel industry, supporting renewable energy projects would be a better direction for public investment (Bérubé, 2016; Suzuki, 2016 October 12).

To strengthen the economic uncertainty frame, the coalition also envisioned "just transition" policies that aimed to break resource communities out of the boom-and-bust cycle by redistributing public funds to sustainable industries. As summarized by a collective of CCPA policy analysts (Cooling et al., 2015 January 28), achieving a just transition requires setting the fossil fuel industry onto a two-to-three-decade wind-down period. This is a challenging task, but with policies encouraging the building of new, green infrastructure as well as the retraining of resource workers, a zero-emission economy could be developed to better serve BC workers and communities. Overall, the framing of BC LNG as an "economic fraud" demonstrates the importance of engaging with economic issues when challenging extractivism.

5.3. Extractivist State and "Wild West" Political Fundraising

Why did the BC Liberal government promote LNG projects so aggressively, given their tenuous economic foundation? Focusing on this question, the anti-LNG discourse coalition scrutinized industry lobbying activities behind LNG-related policymaking, resulting in a "bad governance" frame criticizing LNG development's threats to democracy and government accountability. Discussions following this frame accentuated that in pursuit of launching the LNG industry, the BC Liberal government has acted as an "extractivist state" conspiring with industry stakeholders. Inspired by its neighboring petro-state, Alberta, the BC Liberal government paved the way for LNG development by ignoring and even attacking the legitimate concerns of local communities. Yet, unlike Alberta where the bitumen industry has been a key driver of economic growth for decades, British Columbia's LNG dream was only supported by economic promises that were susceptible to accusations of lack of transparency and democratic policymaking.

The anti-LNG discourse coalition's critical discussions of state-sponsored extractivism centered on tax subsidies and unregulated lobbying activities. To entice foreign LNG investment, the BC Liberal government offered a range of tax incentives, notably reduced LNG taxes and electricity rates.

By problematizing the rationale behind such incentives, coalition members revealed the disparity between the potential prosperity touted by pro-LNG narratives and the actual benefits LNG projects could provide. For example, when Woodfibre LNG became the first BC LNG project to receive preliminary investment approval in late 2016, the Tyee's environmental columnist Andrew Nikiforuk (2016 November 10) harshly criticized the generous "discounts" offered to the project:

> To save face on her outrageous LNG promises, Clark has now offered some significant giveaways to Tanoto [Woodfibre's developer] that every British Columbian will pay for. . . . The government has halved the LNG tax rate to 3.5 per cent – among the lowest in the world and locked it in for 25 years. It granted Woodfibre and other LNG projects an 18-month holiday on carbon taxes. . . . It lowered natural gas royalties to next to nothing and offers the industry nearly $200 million in drilling credits every year. And there will be no sales tax on methane purchases. In addition, the province encouraged Woodfibre on Oct. 25 to pitch the District of Squamish a reduced property tax rate of $2 million instead of the normal mill rate of $8 million to $10 million.
>
> (para. 13–20)

After listing these worrisome numbers, Nikiforuk continued with a rebuttal of LNG proponents' justification of such generosity, pointing out that due to global market changes, government concessions were likely to protect only the interest of private capital:

> British Columbia's LNG advocates may argue that it took such incentives to jumpstart an industry that will produce revenue for the province and jobs for citizens. But with so few jobs (just 100 permanent jobs for the Woodfibre plant) and no guarantee of revenue given all the subsidies, and a global LNG glut, the BC Liberal government has ignored the marketplace and embraced a Soviet model of LNG development. In this special Clark model, taxpayers pay for everything: from the water given to shale gas frackers for free to the electricity provided to energy-gobbling terminals.
>
> (para. 21–23)

Similar to Nikiforuk, My Sea to Sky raised grave concerns about the fairness of Woodfibre's environmental review and subsequent approval. Tracey Saxby (2015 October 27), co-founder of My Sea to Sky, stated that the Woodfibre LNG controversy highlighted the need for more politicized discussions regarding the BC Liberal government's betrayal of broad public interests:

> This approval [of Woodfibre] simply highlights a conflict of interest: how can the public have faith in the integrity of the BC Environmental

Assessment process when the Ministers approving these projects . . . also have a mandate to develop LNG export facilities? Quite simply, we don't. . . . This has not been an open and transparent process, and meaningful community engagement has been limited by short windows for public input, incomplete studies provided by the proponents, and poor advertising of open house events.

(para. 2)

Concurrently with the Woodfibre case, the Pacific NorthWest (PNW) LNG project sparked public outrage over the structural injustice inherent in its public consultation procedure. In July 2015, when the project's primary industry stakeholder, Petronas, reached an initial development agreement with the BC Liberal government, the *National Observer* (Bell, 2015 July 15) warned that the public was given insufficient information, particularly regarding Petronas' history of financial and political scandals. Similarly, Marc Lee (2015b July 14) wrote in the *Tyee*, "what's most disturbing about the BC-Petronas deal is that it's a massive privatization of a public resource for which the people of British Columbia will receive very little in return" (para. 4).

The concerns raised by opponents such as Nikiforuk, Saxby, and Lee exemplified the "bad governance" frame, which, by elaborating how extractivism threatens the integrity of democracy, expanded the range of stakeholders that can be included in the anti-LNG coalition. The framing of the LNG controversy as a political conflict between the state–industry alliance and the public was achieved by disclosing the close relationship between government and industry stakeholders and how it led to unfair policy leanings, as evidenced by the magnitude of LNG-related subsidies. The extensive and substantial tax reductions offered to the BC LNG industry, ranging from carbon tax exemptions to a 25-year fixed royalty regime, had political and economic consequences (Kniewasser, 2017 May 5). Politically, they indicated the BC Liberal Party's poor decision-making and betrayal of the public's desire for a truly green economy. Economically, they resulted in using scarce public dollars to lessen the incentive to reduce carbon pollution.

The anti-LNG discourse coalition attributed the BC Liberal Party's alliance with industry stakeholders to the latter's consistent lobbying efforts and political donations. It affirmed this diagnosis with frequent revelations of pervasive corporate cash in BC politics. The most intense coverage on this issue occurred in January 2017 when a *New York Times* report (Levin, 2017 January 13) depicted British Columbia as the "wild west" of Canadian political cash. Unlike elsewhere in Canada, British Columbia allowed wealthy individuals, corporations, unions, and even foreigners to make large amounts of political donations to provincial parties. For critics of the BC Liberal Party, such cash-for-access "transformed the provincial government into a lucrative business, dominated by special interests that trade donations for political favours, undermining Canada's reputation for functional, consensus-driven democracy" (para. 5).

The *New York Times* report sparked growing public discussions regarding the influence of questionable donations on the BC LNG agenda. By leading these discussions, the anti-LNG discourse coalition articulated the idea of LNG being a threat to democracy's fundamental principles. For instance, the CCPA, through its corporate mapping project, revealed that the fossil fuel industry directed $5.2 million in political donations and 22,000 lobbying contacts to British Columbia's political parties and public officials. Similarly, the environmental organization Wilderness Committee reminded *Tyee* readers that "British Columbia's much-hyped LNG boom has done little except fill the BC Liberal Party's coffers; and in the last four years, the party has received over $1 million from fracking, gas pipeline and LNG companies" (McCartney, 2017 March 14, para. 1). There were also calls for direct forms of civic intervention. The Dogwood Initiative (Sammartino, 2017 February 1), as part of its public campaign calling for banning big money, demanded a corruption inquiry:

> Back to BC where we are still wishing for any sort of cap on donations, and our BC Liberal politicians' response is to laugh at us. We have government decisions being made under the influence of political donations every day.... The difference is that here, our lawmakers say it's legal. . . . What Clark should fear the most is a future government calling a Gomery-style judicial inquiry into her government's fundraising practices. A lot of skeletons pile up in the closets – and behind tinted windows – after a party has been in power for 16 years.
>
> (para. 17–19)

Taken together, these criticisms aimed at directing the public's attention to political scandals and their underlying contradictions, thereby challenging the legitimacy of pro-LNG policies. To complement the discussions on bad governance, the anti-LNG discourse coalition further addressed how activists, through various forms of public resistance, problematized the review processes of numerous LNG proposals. Notably, the persistence of First Nations and their settler allies in saying no to elite outsiders proved to be another powerful frame.

5.4. Social Licence Revoked: Indigenous-led Opposition to LNG Projects

As noted in the previous chapter, many BC First Nations were skeptical of the economic reconciliation promises made by LNG proponents. Driven by this skepticism, Indigenous activists, in close collaboration with their settler allies, actively participated in LNG project public hearings, organized protests and rallies, and disseminated talking points via blog posts and opinion pieces. According to them, there was an intense political struggle regarding

Indigenous sovereignty, identity, injustice, and democratic agency underlying public debates on proposed BC LNG projects.

The anti-LNG discourse coalition supported Indigenous activists' sovereignty claims over un-ceded territories and recognized their persistent blockade of LNG projects (e.g., the Unist'ot'en camp and the Lax Kw'alaams camp) as indicative of a widespread grassroots rejection of state-sponsored extractivism Coalition members' narratives of Indigenous-led opposition centered around the notion of social license, which refers to the resource industries' ongoing efforts to strengthen relationships with communities affected by extractive activities (Gunster & Neubauer, 2019; Murphy-Gregory, 2018; Syn, 2014). Although this concept tends to be criticized because it often legitimizes extractivism, several recent studies have highlighted its radical potential. According to Syn (2014), the metaphor of a license which could be withdrawn any time could empower marginalized communities whose rights have been consistently neglected or violated by governments and corporations. The inherent vagueness of what should be included in public conversations on social license further expands discursive space for environmental activism to contest corporate activities (Murphy-Gregory, 2018).

In British Columbia, for instance, the political conflict surrounding the Northern Gateway Pipeline project was illustrative of opponents promoting extensive debates on why the project should be canceled due to its lack of social license from Indigenous communities (Gunster & Neubauer, 2019). This strategic focus effectively re-articulated the project and its approval process as a continuation of settler colonialism against affected Indigenous communities, and mounting public pressure led to the project's eventual cancelation in November 2016. As the heated debates around Northern Gateway developed in parallel with the provincial government's aggressive push for LNG development, many LNG opponents adopted identical discursive tactics to advance the idea that LNG projects should proceed under affected Indigenous communities' own terms.

During Canadian energy infrastructure controversies, there has been a steady increase of public attention to Indigenous issues since 2014. This trend reflects growing public awareness of the significance of reconciliation and decolonization as a result of decades-long Indigenous activism (Coulthard, 2013 January 4). It was primarily precipitated by the Supreme Court of Canada's decision on the *Tsilhqot'in Nation versus British Columbia* case (Sayers, 2014 July 4). On June 25, 2014, the Supreme Court of Canada issued a ruling supporting the Tsilhqot'in people's claim for the Aboriginal title of their traditional territory. The ruling declared that before approving developments on lands with Aboriginal titles, the Crown has a duty to engage in meaningful consultation with the titleholders. This procedural duty also applies to Indigenous territories with unproven titles in principle. The confirmation of First Nations' exclusive right to decide how to use and control their traditional territories has granted these communities greater leverage when negotiating with corporations.

Prior to the Tsilhqot'in ruling, several First Nations – notably Gitxsan, Fort Nelson, and Wet'suwet'en – had already staged roadblocks and protest camps to obstruct the fast-tracking of fracking and pipeline construction activities that would trespass on their traditional territories (Gillis, 2014 April 16; Sandborn, 2014 February 20). The ruling assertion of Indigenous rights further inspired Indigenous activists and their settler allies to block LNG development through legal claims and civil disobedience. Central to these resistance activities were discourses emphasizing the irreversible harm that resource extraction would cause to the sustainability of Indigenous life. Treaty 8 First Nations, for instance, viewed the BC Liberal government's aggressive push for the Site C dam project as an unacceptable breach of treaty duties:

> Treaty 8 First Nations in BC are vehemently opposed to BC Hydro's plans to build a third massive dam [Site C] on the Peace River that would be . . . in direct contravention of the 1899 treaty: destroy land now used for hunting, fishing and collecting medicinal plants. . . . The treaty states First Nations have the right to continue with their way of life "for as long as the sun shines, the grass grows and the rivers flow", but with massive resource development in the area, the sun, grass and rivers are all at risk and Site C is the final straw.
>
> (Lavoie, 2014 July 3, para. 4–8)

The reference to the 1899 treaty directed the discussions on Site C towards future visions of settler-Indigenous relations. The story then cited Treaty 8 Tribal Association Chief Liz Logan to highlight a major concern amongst local Indigenous communities, namely mercury poisoning of fish:

> With high levels of methylmercury in fish because of rotting vegetation from the previous two dams, fishing is restricted and ungulates, such as caribou, are being destroyed by the major projects, said Treaty 8 Tribal Association Chief Liz Logan. . . . "We have become the cash register for the province . . . and now our way of life is going to be interfered with again".
>
> (para. 9–11)

Logan's concern should not be understood simply as a food safety issue. In a follow-up *DeSmog Canada* report (Linnitt, 2015 May 13), Chief Roland Willson from the West Moberly First Nation provided detailed explanations of the important meanings of fishing and consumption of salmon to his community and that maintaining both were crucial for passing Indigenous ways of life to future generations. Following this argument, Indigenous activists' disagreement about Site C had significant political implications for decolonization.

Treaty 8 First Nations were not alone in opposing Site C's detrimental social, environmental, and cultural impacts. Environmental organizations such as the David Suzuki Foundation and the Sierra Club BC and non-Indigenous residents across the Peace Valley region also joined the legal actions against the project's approval. In other protests, the formation of an alliance uniting Indigenous and settler voices also emerged, and its construction of collectivity helped position the push for LNG exports as an undemocratic policy agenda against the will of the people.

The most remarkable case showing the power of Indigenous resistance occurred in May 2015, when the Lax Kw'alaams First Nation near Prince Rupert declined to give consent in exchange for more than $1 billion in promised economic benefits from Petronas, the primary investor of the PNW LNG proposal (Jang, 2015 May 13). To the surprise of LNG proponents, the decisive factor leading to such a decision was the project's impact on the juvenile wild salmon habitat in the Skeena River's Flora Bank, located close to the proposed LNG site on Lelu Island. The economic benefits of salmon fishing are incomparable to the incoming Petronas investment, yet many Lax Kw'alaams members were furious about the exclusion of salmon's cultural significance in the project's impact assessment process. Ian Gill (2015 May 9), a reporter for *Tyee*, followed the community's voting process, and his in-depth report provides insight into the mentalities of some members who voted to prioritize nature and traditional knowledge over economic benefits:

> In Lax Kw'alaams on Tuesday night, those savvy band members sided with the salmon. "I will never, ever give up the Skeena River for money", one participant said, "there is far too much at stake". I spoke with one elder . . . who said she was relieved that such an "outlandish proposal" was voted down on Tuesday night. The vote: 181 opposed, zero in favour. . . . Far from this current exercise being a breakthrough that shows how to get the job done with testy aboriginal communities, it might yet turn out to be a textbook example of how not to.
>
> (para. 25)

The Lax Kw'alaams members' determination, according to Gill, had far-reaching implications for Crown–Indigenous relations in Canada:

> It clearly confounds companies that they can't just buy a social licence in the same way they can get a business licence or an export licence, but that won't stop them from trying. And, as we are witnessing with the Site C dam development, eventually the government will just invoke what it considers to be the superior interests of the Crown over the constitutionally enshrined and court-confirmed rights of Canada's First Nations. . . . But the stern resolve of the people of Lax Kw'alaams is of a piece with their

ancient history, and in standing up for their rights, they are making modern history too. There's more than a glimmer of justice in that.

(para. 26–27)

Recognizing that the state–industry alliance would not easily give up, the Lax Kw'alaams First Nation initiated follow-up actions to safeguard their ancestral heritage. Following the vote, a group of dedicated Lax Kw'alaams activists set up a protest camp on Lelu Island to monitor and block early test drillings. Learning from the Tsilhqot'in Nation's experience, the community also filed an aboriginal title claim to Lelu Island and Flora Bank in order to bolster the political significance of their resistance. Then in January 2016, Lax Kw'alaams hosted a two-day Salmon Nation Summit, which led to the signing of the Lelu Declaration by a coalition of Indigenous leaders, local residents, and federal and provincial politicians (from the opposition NDP). As a milestone affirming the unity of the anti-LNG discourse coalition, the declaration demanded permanent protection of the Skeena estuary from industrial development, given the area's ecological significance and special meanings for Indigenous culture.

In short, Indigenous resistance enabled the anti-LNG discourse coalition to frame LNG development as a continuation of settler colonialism. Accordingly, the protection of Indigenous lands and waters strengthened the political legitimacy of the anti-LNG movement. As Chief Na'Moks from the Wet'suwet'en First Nation commented on the Lelu declaration:

Once again First Nations are being forced to take action because the government refuses to obey the laws of the land. We are salmon people and if we don't defend Flora Bank, there will be no protection for our salmon. The salmon is who we are, and without them we lose our identity and our future.

(Gill, 2016 January 25, para. 20)

Although the majority of BC First Nations maintained their opposition throughout 2012–2017, noticeable internal disagreements emerged under the intensive lobbying of the state–industry alliance, which managed to sign benefits agreements with several First Nations and transformed them into LNG advocates joining the pro-LNG civil group First Nations LNG Alliance. Meanwhile, in communities where the anti-LNG sentiment remained strong, some elected leaders gradually softened their opposition. Two months after the signing of the Lelu Declaration, Lax Kw'alaam's newly elected mayor, John Helin, suggested that he was open to supporting the PNW LNG terminal if additional environmental protection measures were taken (McCarthy, 2016 March 18). Mr. Helin's statement, however, received strong backlash from some Lax Kw'alaam hereditary leaders, who insisted that elected officials alone could not make the decision on behalf of the Lax Kw'alaam people. There was a similar case in the Gitxsan Nation. The community was once a vocal opponent to TransCanada's proposed Prince Rupert Gas Transmission Pipeline, which would transport northeast British Columbia's natural gas to the proposed LNG terminal on Lelu Island (Gillis, 2014 August 28). Yet in 2016, eight Gitxsan hereditary chiefs gave consent to the pipeline. A Discourse Media investigation (Jang, 2017 February 10) later revealed that these chiefs were subject to accusations of corruption. In this context, it was imperative that the anti-LNG discourse coalition articulate viable alternatives to resource extraction.

5.5. Chapter Conclusion

This chapter has examined four prominent discursive frames constructed by LNG opponents to explicate the substantive concerns surrounding the proposed BC LNG sector's multiple adverse impacts. The anti-LNG storyline features public denunciations of shale gas as a looming threat to air, water, landscape, human health, and even the interests of the provincial economy and democratic governance. The chapter has also illustrated how the storyline evolved from late 2011 to mid-2017, with a confluence of environmental voices later escalating into a radical counter-discourse exposing industry–state co-optation and the hypocrisy of extractivism. Although the chapter has focussed on arguments made by well-known LNG critics, the real strength of the anti-LNG discourse coalition lies in the diversity of its membership and the determination expressed by the protest rallies it organized.

Turning to the specific content of the anti-LNG storyline, the environmental degradation frame did not aggressively confront public imperatives such as economic growth and job security, which provided the pro-LNG storyline with powerful plausibility. Nonetheless, LNG opponents attempted to increase the frame's acceptability by elaborating on environmental risks in relation to rural BC residents' daily experiences. This frame was particularly persuasive when it was collectively articulated by elite environmental organizations and ordinary citizens. The widespread anger over the BC Liberal government's extractivist policies turned many people into "accidental activists", and it was challenging for the pro-LNG coalition to dispel such grassroots opposition. Issues such as water safety, loss of arable land (due to Site C), and threat to salmon habitat resonated with the BC public, as evidenced by the impressive turnouts at related rallies. My Sea to Sky, for instance, was able to gather more than 18,000 signatures for its petition against Woodfibre LNG via a series of public campaigns (the Howe Sound Petition, n.d.).

The unmasking of shale gas's bridge fuel designation was well perceived amongst citizens with greater skepticism about the governing party's ability to shield public interests from capitalist appropriation. From the perspective of discursive dynamics, the environmental degradation frame sought to dis-integrate the pro-LNG storyline by challenging the credibility of its leader: the BC Liberal Party. That said, this frame did not become well perceived in resource-dependent communities and was unable to lessen their residents' (e.g., Fort St. John) obsession with LNG development.

The frame on fossil fuel lock-in and economic uncertainty was initially peripheral but later gained prominence when the Asian LNG price collapse fully exposed the fragile economic basis of BC LNG's business model. The frame's plausibility derived from research reports by progressive think tanks, which cast doubt on fossil fuel boosterism by interpreting data from the fossil fuel industry's market analyses. The presence of economic critiques is truly unique and interesting, which points to the potential of employing mainstream economic wisdom to resist the expansion of extreme carbon. In light of the frequent intertextual references to these critiques in anti-LNG narratives, questions surrounding BC LNG's economic viability played a significant part in the anti-LNG campaign, and their credibility amongst ordinary citizens – even those from resource-dependent communities – was arguably better than anti-fracking messages. Public attention to these economic critiques is largely determined by relevant news coverage, and this topic is addressed in the next chapter.

It is inspiring to note that opposition to LNG also evolved into broader discussions on democratic governance and social licence, which highlighted a lack of transparency, accountability, and citizen input. Such discussions focussed on policymaking surrounding LNG's regulation and development. This process of politicization indicates that extreme carbon has become "an object of democratic debate between conflicting yet legitimate politi-cal projects, between conflicting, yet legitimate, social actors, or more specifically, politico-ideological conflict between alternative futures" (Pep-ermans & Maeseele, 2014, p. 224). LNG opponents were compelled to rely on regional populist support to criticize industry–state co-optation in light of the BC Liberal government's concessions in environmental stewardship and embrace of shale gas extraction and export. The discussions of democratic governance and social licence improved the trustworthiness and relevance of the anti-LNG discourse coalition among the general public since the idea of local communities threatened by the intrusive actions of government and industry elites tended to fall on receptive ears usually distant from civil disobedience.

This chapter has explained LNG opponents' efforts to move beyond the conventional "jobs versus the environment" dichotomy by exploring the details of the anti-LNG storyline. With a grasp of both the pro- and anti-LNG discourse coalitions' discursive strategies, the following chapter will analyze how the two competing narratives influenced Canadian media coverage of the BC LNG controversy.

References

Ball, D. P. (2014, December 16). Site C dam approved: A tyee reader. *The Tyee*. Retrieved May 14, 2018, from https://thetyee.ca

BC Ministry of Energy and Mines. (2012, February 03). *Liquified natural gas: A strategy for British Columbia's newest industry*. https://vufind.llbc.leg.bc.ca/

Bérubé, A. (2016, November 15). Fossil fuel subsidies are the elephant in the room. *Canada's National Observer*. www.nationalobserver.com

Bell, W. (2015, July 15). As scandal rocks Malaysian government, B.C. pushes LNG deal with state-owned gas giant. *National Observer*. from https://www.nationalobserver.com

Bell, W. (2017, August 9). Site C: A 21st century Titanic. *Canada's National Observer*. www.nationalobserver.com

Cooling, K., Lee, M., Daub, S., & Singer, J. (2015, January 28). *Making a just transition (commentary)*. Canadian Centre for Policy Alternatives. www.policyalternatives.ca

Coulthard, G. (2013, January 4). Placing #IdleNoMore in historical context. *The Tyee*. Retrieved May 14, 2018, from www.thetyee.ca

Dodge, J., & Metze, T. (2017). Hydraulic fracturing as an interpretive policy problem: Lessons on energy controversies in Europe and the U.S.A. *Journal of Environmental Policy & Planning*, *19*(1), 1–13, https://doi.org/10.1080/1523908X.2016.1277947

Eagle, R. (2017, March 23). Four decades and counting: A brief history of the Site C dam. *DeSmog Canada*. www.desmog.ca

Fox, J. (Director). (2010). *Gasland* [Motion picture]. International WOW Company.

Gilchrist, E. (2015, June 12). It's official: Site C Dam could power fracking operations in Northeast BC. *DeSmog Canada*. www.desmog.ca

Gill, I. (2015, May 5). No wealth, No justice in $1 billion LNG offer to First Nation band. *The Tyee*. www.thetyee.ca.

Gill, I. (2016, January 25). Lelu Declaration a major wrench in hardhat Premier's LNG plans. *The Tyee*. www.thetyee.ca.

Gillis, D. (2014, April 16). BC LNG faces growing First Nations opposition. *The Common Sense Canadian*. http://commonsensecanadian.ca

Gillis, D. (2014, August 28). Gitxsan clan closes territory to LNG, blockades Petronas pipeline. *The Common Sense Canadian*. http://commonsensecanadian.ca

Gunster, S., & Neubauer, R. J. (2019). (De)legitimating extractivism: The shifting politics of social licence. *Environmental Politics*, *28*(4), 707–726. https://doi.org/10.1080/09644016.2018.1507290

Hoekstra, G. (2016, March 23). Poll shows support for LNG slipping, dislike for fracking increasing. *The Vancouver Sun*. https://vancouversun.com

Horne, M., & MacNab, J. (2014, October 27). *LNG and climate change: The global context*. Pembina Institute. www.pembina.org/

Hughes, J. D. (2015, May). *A clear look at BC LNG: Energy security, environmental implications and economic potential*. Canadian Centre for Policy Alternatives. www.policyalternatives.ca

Jang, B. (2015, May 13). BC first nations group rejects $1-billion offer for LNG venture. *The Globe and Mail*. www.theglobeandmail.com/

Jang, T. (2017, February 10). Investigation traces flow of public money into hands of BC chiefs in exchange for LNG support. *Canada's National Observer*. www.nationalobserver.com/

Klein, S. (2015, December 28). Admitting a post-Paris truth: British Columbia's LNG pipe dream is over. *Policy Note.* www.policynote.ca/

Kniewasser, M. (2017, May 5). Six troubling subsidies that support British Columbia's LNG industry. *DeSmog Canada.* www.desmog.ca

Lavoie, J. (2014, May 27). The 7.9 billion-dollar question: Is the Site C Dam's electricity destined for LNG industry? *DeSmog Canada.* www.desmog.ca

Lavoie, J. (2014, July 3). Site C Dam is final straw for British Columbia's Treaty 8 First Nations. *DeSmog Canada.* https://www.desmog.ca

Leahy, S. (2013, March 14). Blame Canada part 2: Canada's plan to get rich by trashing the climate. *DeSmog Canada.* www.desmog.ca

Leahy, S. (2013, May 8). Unreported emissions from natural gas blow up British Columbia's climate action plan – British Columbia's carbon footprint likely 25% greater than reported. *DeSmog Canada.* www.desmog.ca

Lee, M. (2012, February 8). Comparing two carbon bombs: LNG plants vs Enbridge pipeline. *Policy Note.* www.policynote.ca

Lee, M. (2014). LNG: British Columbia's quest for a new staple industry. In J. Stanford (Ed.), *The staple theory @ 50* (pp. 80–83). Canadian Centre for Policy Alternatives.

Lee, M. (2015a). *LNG and employment in British Columbia.* Canadian Centre for Policy Alternatives. www.policyalternatives.ca

Lee, M. (2015b July 14). Just how bad is British Columbia's LNG deal with Petronas? *The Tyee.* www.thetyee.ca

Lee, M. (2015c, November 12). Five LNG whoppers. *Policy Note.* www.policynote.ca/

Levin, D. (2017, January 13). British Columbia: The 'wild west' of Canadian political cash. *The New York Times.* www.nytimes.com

Linnitt, C. (2015, May 13). First nations chief fears site C will increase mercury poisoning of fish. *DeSmog Canada.* www.desmog.ca

Matthews J., & Hansen, A. (2018). Fracturing debate? A review of research on media coverage of "fracking". *Frontiers in Communication, 3,* item 41. https://doi.org/10.3389/fcomm.2018.00041

McCartney, P. (2016). *LNG: A dirty secret on the west coast.* The Wilderness Committee. www.wildernesscommittee.org

McCartney, P. (2017, March 14). What $1 million in fossil fuel money buys in BC politics. *The Tyee.* www.thetyee.ca

McCarthy, S. (2016, March 18). Lax Kw'alaam Band gives green light to Pacific North West – with conditions. *The Globe and Mail.* www.theglobeandmail.com

Murphy-Gregory, H. (2018). Governance via persuasion: Environmental NGOs and the social licence to operate. *Environmental Politics, 27*(2), 320–340. https://doi.org/10.1080/09644016.2017.1373429

Nikiforuk, A. (2016, November 10). British Columbia's LNG fraud. *The Tyee.* www.thetyee.ca

Olive, A., & Delshad, A. B. (2017). Fracking and framing: A comparative analysis of media coverage of hydraulic fracturing in Canadian and U.S. newspapers. *Environmental Communication, 11*(6), 784–799, https://doi.org/10.1080/17524032.2016.1275734

Parfitt, B. (2011, November 9). *Fracking up our water, hydro power and climate: British Columbia's reckless pursuit of shale gas.* Canadian Centre for Policy Alternatives. www.policyalternatives.ca

Parfitt, B. (2016, February 4). Ever wondered why Site C rhymes with LNG? *DeSmog Canada*. www.desmog.ca

Parfitt, B., & Hughes, D. (2014, February 24). Where will all the water come from LNG? *The Province*. https://theprovince.com

Pepermans, Y., & Maeseele, P. (2014). Democratic debate and mediated discourses on climate change: From consensus to de/politicization, Journal of Environmental Communication, 8(2), 216–232. https://doi.org/10.1080/17524032.2014.906482

Prystupa, M. (2016, February 23). Site C is a climate-change disaster, says Suzuki. *The Tyee*. https://thetyee.ca

Rankin, E., & McElroy, J. (2017, April 11). Fact check: Promises, promises – last election's 'epic fail'. *CBC News*. www.cbc.ca

Sandborn, T. (2014, February 20). Camped for three years, aboriginal blockaders vow to stop northern LNG pipeline. *The Tyee*. www.thetyee.ca.

Saxby, T. (2015, October 27). Woodfibre LNG may have govt's rubber stamp, but not social license. *The Common Sense Canadians*. http://commonsensecanadian.ca

Sayers, J. (2014, July 4). How the Tsilhqot'in decision changes business in British Columbia. *The Tyee*. www.thetyee.ca

Sammartino, L. (2017, February 1). BC is overdue for a corruption inquiry. *The Dogwood Initiative*. https://dogwoodbc.ca

Shaffer, M. (2016, November 16). Why should British Columbians pay power bills for LNG industry? *The Tyee*. www.thetyee.ca

Sierra Club BC. (2017). *Public inquiry needed to properly investigate deep social and environmental harms of fracking, coalition says*. https://sierraclub.bc.ca

Suzuki, D. (2015, January 06). Energy shift requires shift in conversation. *DeSmog Canada*. Retrieved May 12, 2018, from www.desmog.ca

Suzuki, D. (2016, October 12). We can't dig our way out of the fossil fuels hole. *DeSmog Canadc*. www.desmog.ca

Syn, J. (2014). The social license: Empowering communities and a better way forward. *Social Epistemology*, 28(3–4) 318–339. https://doi.org/10.1080/02691728.2014.922640

The Howe Sound Petition (n.c.). https://myseatosky.org/take-action/sign-the-petition-to-stop-woodfibre-lng/

6   Debating BC LNG in Canadian Media

The two competing storylines explicated in the preceding chapters are diverse and intricate, comprising economic, political, environmental, and moral claims that are intertwined. On the one hand, LNG proponents argued that expanding shale gas extraction and launching LNG exports to Asia would bring substantial economic benefits to British Columbia and contribute to the reduction of global greenhouse gas emissions. LNG opponents, on the other hand, were concerned about the LNG industry's fragile economic foundation and the devastating social and environmental effects it would have on British Columbia's coastal and interior communities.

Although the identification of both storylines has yielded critical insights into the stakeholders' divergent ideological positions on the role of extractivism in the economic future of British Columbia, further analysis is required to determine how the discursive struggles between LNG proponents and opponents influenced media coverage of the BC LNG controversy. From late 2011 to mid-2017, regional and national media paid sustained attention to proposed BC LNG projects. Cognizant of the media's significant impact on public opinion, both pro- and anti-LNG discourse coalitions have sought to promote their viewpoints by influencing relevant news coverage.

To assess the effectiveness of each discourse coalition in shaping the Canadian news agenda, this chapter presents a comparative analysis of media coverage of the Pacific NorthWest LNG project (PNW), using the data collection and analysis methods outlined in Chapter 1. This project, with an eye-catching cost estimate of $36 billion CAD, was widely regarded as the flagship project of the upcoming BC LNG industry, and its coverage in the media was a crucial aspect of BC LNG public discourse between 2014 and 2017. In September 2016, after lengthy negotiations over taxation and environmental concerns, the project cleared all regulatory hurdles. Ten months later, however, Petronas, which led the consortium of investors, decided to cancel the project, which dealt a severe blow to the Canadian fossil fuel industry.

The anti-LNG discourse coalition applauded the cancellation and viewed it as a clear indication of the economic, social, and environmental absurdity of BC LNG projects. The pro-LNG discourse coalition, in contrast, placed the

DOI: 10.4324/9781003350620-6

blame on "ongoing sabotage" by environmentalists and the formation of an "anti-development" New Democratic Party (NDP) minority government in British Columbia following the 2017 provincial election. Yet, to what extent did the "jobs killed by environmentalists" accusation reflect the dynamics of public debates regarding BC LNG? To find out, the chapter explores:

(1) How did Canadian news outlets cover the policy negotiations and public debates preceding the cancellation of PNW?
(2) According to relevant news coverage, what were the primary points of contention between PNW proponents and opponents?
(3) What distinguished public, commercial, and independent media in their mediation of public discussions on the BC LNG controversy?

6.1. Quantitative Content Analysis Findings

The current comparative study focuses on PNW-related news articles and opinion pieces that appeared in six Canadian news outlets: CBC News, the *Globe and Mail*, the *National Post*, the *Vancouver Sun*, the *Tyee*, and *Canada's National Observer*. They represent public, commercial, and independent news actors in the Canadian media landscape. They are not unbiased institutions that merely inform the public about various stakeholder claims. Each outlet has its own biases that make it structurally more receptive to the arguments of particular stakeholders. Following the methodology outlined in Chapter 1, news items collected from the target media were analyzed using a mixed-methods approach that incorporated both quantitative content analysis and qualitative discourse analysis.

The quantitative content analysis reveals three different approaches taken by the media outlets in reporting the PNW LNG controversy: (1) Postmedia leaned toward industry stakeholders and frequently played a dual role as both an advocate for extractivism and a conservative critic of LNG opponents; (2) CBC News and the *Globe and Mail* were also pro-industry, but they were also vocal about PNW's inherent economic and environmental risks; (3) the *Tyee* and *Canada's National Observer* sided with LNG opponents by advocating for the rejection of PNW.

Table 6.1 presents the yearly distribution of news items featuring PNW in each media source. The peaks in media coverage indicate that initial media attention to PNW was triggered by the negotiations between the Petronas-led consortium and the BC government. Following multiple warnings about the project's environmental impacts in 2015 and afterwards, public contestation over whether it should be approved gradually mounted into a high-profile controversy. The high monthly average of 2014 ($N = 21.5$) consists mainly of articles from the commercial media's business sections. Relevant coverage from CBC News, the *Tyee*, and *Canada's National Observer* later surged during 2015–2016, even though their numbers of published news items remained

Table 6.1 Yearly Distribution of PNW News Items

	CBC in % (N = 67)	Globe and Mail in % (N = 196)	Postmedia in % (N = 284)	Tyee in % (N = 44)	National Observer in % (N = 27)	Monthly Average
2014 (09–12)	7.5	14.8	16.9	9.1	0	21.5
2015	22.4	36.7	39.1	25	14.8	17.75
2016	50.7	33.2	31.3	34.1	37	17.75
2017 (01–08)	19.4	15.3	12.7	31.8	48.2	13.25
Total (%)	100	100	100	100	100	

Table 6.2 PNW News Items by Content Type

Media	General Sections		Business Sections	
	News	Opinion	News	Opinion
CBC News (N = 67)	54	3	9	1
Globe and Mail (N = 196)	90	17	78	11
Postmedia (N = 284)	51	69	143	21
Tyee (N = 44)	22	22	0	0
National Observer (N = 27)	15	12	0	0
Total (N = 618)	232	123	230	33

considerably smaller than the commercial newspapers. In 2017, the mainstream outlets' attention to PNW dropped considerably compared to the previous two years. The independent media, however, did not follow this trend: both the *Tyee* and *National Observer* published substantial proportions of their PNW coverage (31.8% and 48.2%, respectively) in 2017. A closer look at news items published in this year demonstrates a notable surge of independent media stories supporting activists' resistance to the federal government's conditional approval of PNW.

Table 6.2 outlines the distribution of news items in each content type. In both general and business sections, the surveyed media yielded a mix of news and opinion pieces. Postmedia was the most prolific (*N* = 284), followed by the *Globe and Mail* (*N* = 196). In the case of Postmedia, its extensive PNW coverage mainly consists of news and opinion pieces appearing in various business sections (e.g., Financial Post, FP Energy, FP Investing, Western Business, etc.). The *Globe and Mail* followed a similar distribution pattern, except for one notable difference: it had a substantively higher proportion of PNW coverage (90 out of 196, 45.92%) in general news sections than Postmedia (51 out of 284, 17.96%). Postmedia published the greatest number of business news articles (*N* = 143), many of which provided detailed updates on Petronas' negotiations with provincial and federal ministries responsible for regulating natural gas development. It also published the most opinion pieces in both general ($N = 69$) and business ($N = 21$) sections, reflecting the determination of its columnists and commentators to influence the policy and public agendas of PNW. In short, the results presented in Tables 6.1 and 6.2 suggest a process of politicization wherein intensifying public debates transformed PNW into a political controversy outside of business circles.

The frequencies of different media content over time (Table 6.3) reveal two additional patterns. First, PNW stories appearing in general news sections were dwarfed by those in business sections in 2014; however, this trend shifted over subsequent years. Between 2016 and 2017, significantly more general news stories were published than business news stories. Second, opinion pieces targeting general readers outnumbered those targeting business readers over the 36-month period. This brief media chronology demonstrates that PNW-related media peaks were closely related to the project's review and decision-making process.

Table 6.4 outlines how the media approached the PNW controversy, as indicated by the frequencies of their publications from economic, political, and environmental perspectives. Whilst CBC News and the *Globe* and *Mail* achieved roughly equal distribution amongst the three perspectives, Postmedia focused heavily on economics, with 47.2% of its news items primarily addressing this perspective. By comparison, political issues were the overarching focus of both independent media.

Table 6.3 Different Types of Media Content over Time

Year	General Sections		Business Sections	
	News	Opinion	News	Opinion
2014 (09–12)	19	15	49	3
2015	71	39	95	8
2016	94	36	71	12
2017 (01–08)	43	33	15	10
Total	232	123	230	33

Table 6.4 Distribution of News Items by Thematic Perspective

Perspective	CBC News in % (N = 67)	Globe & Mail in % (N = 196)	Postmedia in % (N = 284)	Tyee in % (N = 44)	National Observer in % (N = 27)
Economics	34.4	35.7	47.2	20.5	7.4
Politics	32.8	33.2	29.2	63.6	55.6
Environment	32.8	31.1	23.6	15.9	37
Total (%)	100	100	100	100	100

Table 6.5 provides additional information regarding the frequency of various themes in each perspective. Postmedia's prioritization of economic themes was mainly driven by its extensive coverage ($N = 67$, 23.6% out of 284) of Petronas's prolonged negotiation with provincial and federal governments over LNG taxation and project cost. It also published the most news items attacking government interference and environmentalism ($N = 21$, 7.4% out of 284). As for independent media, both strongly criticized the BC LNG agenda with multiple news items explicating its policy failure (N of *Tyee* = 18, 40.9% out of 44; N of *Canada's National Observer* = 6, 22.2% out of 27). Meanwhile, the relatively consistent percentage of news items addressing project uncertainty across the mainstream media point to the persistency of PNW's inherent business risks.

Table 6.5 also illustrates that public opinion was the most frequent theme featured in political news items. To examine the media's framing of mixed public attitudes toward PNW, I conducted follow-up coding of the "Public Opinion" theme and divided it into three sub-themes: community support, opposition, and division (Table 6.6). Over 50% of media coverage on public opinion focused on public resistance to PNW, especially from Indigenous communities. Postmedia was the only media source to provide significant coverage (over 30%) of community support for the project. In contrast, both independent media prioritized the reporting of continuing community resistance

Table 6.5 Thematic Distribution of News Items

Theme	CBC News in % (N = 67)	Globe & Mail in % (N = 196)	Postmedia in % (N = 284)	Tyee in % (N = 44)	National Observer in % (N = 27)
Economics					
1.1. Negotiation	13.4	16.9	23.6	0	0
1.2. Economic Development	6	9.7	9.9	6.8	0
1.3. Project Uncertainty	14.9	9.2	13.7	13.6	7.4
Politics					
2.1. Public Opinion	31.4	24.5	16.5	20.5	25.9
2.2. Disputes from Opposition Parties	0	5.6	5.3	2.3	7.4
2.3. Extractivist Policy Failure	0	1	0	40.9	22.2
2.4. Conservative Attacks	1.5	2	7.4	0	0
Environment					
3.1. Review and Regulation	17.9	25	15.1	0	0
3.2. Alarming Impacts	14.9	6.1	8.5	15.9	37.1
Total (%)	100	100	100	100	100

Table 6.6 Public Opinions on PNW

Public Opinion	CBC News in % (N = 21)	Globe & Mail in % (N = 48)	Postmedia in % (N = 47)	Tyee in % (N = 9)	National Observer in % (N = 7)
Support	14.3	22.9	34	0	0
Opposition	66.7	52.1	55.3	88.9	57.1
Division	19	25 1	10.7	11.1	42.9
Total (%)	100	100	100	100	100

to PNW, with no attention paid to PNW's community support. Based on the differences between media outlets identified in Tables 6.4 to 6.6, the following sections provide a qualitative analysis of their framing of the Pacific Northwest and interactions with proponents and opponents of LNG development.

6.2. Public Media: BC LNG as a Prolonged Controversy

According to Bennett (1995), traditional media and their political reporting are under the constant influence of three normative orders: (1) economic norms in the business operation of news organizations, (2) political norms in the role of journalism in politics, and (3) professional norms in the journalistic tenets of objectivity and fairness. Among these normative orders, of particular relevance to the current study are the professional norms that guide journalists in their daily practice to prioritize elite over citizen input, adopt authoritative writing styles, and pursue balanced reporting. Based on these criteria, CBC News acted as a quintessentially traditional media organization throughout its PNW coverage. It published a total of only four PNW-related opinion pieces over the surveyed period, all of which were written by CBC journalists instead of external commentators. This cautious approach clearly suggests CBC's unwillingness to intervene in public debates over PNW.

Whilst the basic tone of CBC's PNW stories relied heavily on industry and government sources, it also made reasonable efforts to balance pro-industry voices with dissenting voices from scientists, environmental organizations, and social groups. For example, CBC's report on the federal environmental approval of PNW (Tasker, 2016a September 27) relied primarily on the official announcement from federal Environmental Minister Catherine McKenna, thereby reinforcing the federal government's confidence that the approval was based on a stringent environmental review process and extensive consultations with affected Indigenous communities. To back McKenna's claims, the report also drew on information from the Canadian Environmental Assessment Agency. It then shifted to the response issued by Adnan Zainal Abidin, president of PNW LNG. Finally, to adhere to the tenet of balanced reporting, the report ended with critics from federal opposition parties as well as mixed local reactions to the approval. Similar sourcing patterns structured most CBC stories on PNW.

CBC's consideration of journalistic objectivity led it to adopt discursive frames from both pro- and anti-LNG storylines. According to its coverage, BC LNG projects were indeed controversial, with both proponents and opponents presenting reasonable arguments. This relatively objective stance makes CBC a useful source for exploring the PNW timeline and the identification of major points of contention. The qualitative analysis of CBC's coverage of PNW reveals the following key developments during the project's negotiation and review process, which inform the analysis of more ideologically charged texts published by commercial and independent media in later sections.

The initial surge of media attention to PNW in late 2014 was triggered by talks between Petronas and the BC Liberal government concerning the tax scheme of LNG exports. These early reports discussed British Columbia's lack of competitiveness in the wake of Asia's falling LNG prices, a key threat to the unity of the pro-LNG discourse coalition. During this period, Petronas made multiple appearances in news headlines (e.g., Lus, 2014 October 6), warning that PNW would not proceed unless BC granted tax relief to compensate for potential revenue loss. With discursive support from pro-industry columnists and commentators, notably those appearing in the commercial media, Petronas's blackmail tactics proved to be effective: although the BC Liberal government strove to maintain stakeholder and public confidence in LNG's long-term economic viability, it eventually conceded and granted fixed royalty and tax rates to PNW via a precedent-setting agreement with Petronas ("Rich Coleman pushes for LNG project", 2015 July 14).

In the meantime, a political challenge gradually emerged near Lelu Island, the project's designated site. In May 2015, news broke that members of the Lax Kw'alaams First Nation had overwhelmingly declined to give their consent to Petronas's plan to locate PNW on Lelu Island, their traditional territory ("Lax Kw'alaams Band reject $1B LNG deal", 2015 May 13). Following this unexpected rejection, Lax Kw'alaams members, under the leadership of several hereditary chiefs, set up a long-term protest camp to block development activities related to PNW. Accordingly, Indigenous opposition, as well as PNW's environmental impacts, gradually became the focal issues of media coverage. For its part, CBC adopted arguments made by both LNG proponents and critics to highlight the sense of division: different stakeholders held contrasting opinions on whether PNW had garnered sufficient Indigenous consent and minimized environmental risks to an acceptable level (e.g., "Lelu Island LNG project divides First Nations", 2015 November 12; "Petronas LNG terminal set in salmon's Grand Central Station", 2015 August 7). In the face of mounting pressure from environmental and Indigenous groups, the Clark government did not back off. Instead, it defended its commitment to LNG with the "clean fossil fuel" branding of shale gas (Meuse, 2016 May 30). Yet, this strategy proved relatively ineffective in the CBC coverage because it was overwhelmed by the voices of climate change experts and activists who cited scientific evidence to call for a halt to PNW (e.g., Bickis, 2016 August 24).

With the federal environmental assessment being the only remaining regulatory hurdle, the PNW controversy expanded beyond the provincial level, and the assessment became the central focus of PNW news throughout 2016. After a lengthy review process, the federal Liberal government led by Justin Trudeau approved PNW with 190 legally binding conditions in September 2016 (Tasker, 2016a September 27). In response, CBC offered extensive coverage (e.g., Meuse, 2016 October 3; Wherry, 2016 September 28) of different responses to this approval, focussing on how it triggered broad public debates over issues such as environmental protection, Indigenous communities' relationships with Canada's energy sector, and LNG's uncertain future in light of the global market downturn. As for discursive frames, the CBC stories reiterated the federal government's belief in balancing economic benefits and environmental impacts via administrative means on the one hand and LNG critics' condemnation of the federal government's compromise to the fossil fuel industry on the other.

Although the federal approval excited LNG proponents since it offered a much-needed positive step for the stalled BC LNG agenda, investors' reactions were more reserved. Whilst the approval was widely discussed in Canadian media, the Petronas-led consortium kept silent on whether it would proceed with an FID. Instead, it launched a comprehensive project review to reassess the project's viability (Tasker, 2016b September 29). The consortium's ambiguous stance, combined with continuing market pressure in Asia and court challenges from Indigenous and environmental groups, added uncertainty to PNW's prospects. The eventual cancellation of PNW came in July 2017. CBC's reporting of it followed Petronas's statement to define it as a business decision due mainly to unfavorable market conditions (Ghoussoub, 2017 July 25) CBC's report also noted that the cancellation brought both fear and happiness to British Columbia's Northern communities since their members held divided opinions on LNG (Kurjata, 2017 July 25).

In sum, the overview of PNW's chronology in CBC News highlights three major points of contention between LNG proponents and opponents: (1) British Columbia's lack of competitiveness as a result of being a latecomer to the global LNG race, (2) the provincial public's divided responses to LNG development, and (3) the provincial and federal governments' progressive yet extractive approach to the conflict between economic development and environmental protection. In these key debates, CBC News played its national broadcaster role by trying to function as an objective information intermediary, providing its readers facts and opinion from both sides of the controversy. In contrast, the ideological leanings of commercial and independent media outlets led them to consistently favor pro- or anti-LNG sources, perspectives, and arguments, which, as the following two sections demonstrate, contributed to the polarization of pro- and anti-LNG narratives.

6.3. Commercial Media: Between Fossil Fuel Advocates and Business Risk Analysts

The *Globe and Mail* and Postmedia's PNW coverage demonstrated three notable features. The first was their business sections, which were rich in content and served the interests of industry and business professionals with specialized information. The elite/expert sources cited in such business stories could be further divided into fossil fuel advocates and business risk analysts. Whilst the former group was concerned mainly with defending the economic interests of Canadian fossil fuel stakeholders, the latter attended to the competitiveness of Canada in global energy markets. Second, the journalistic objectivity followed by the commercial media in news reporting did not apply to their opinion pieces, which in the current case took an evident pro-industry stance and presented a discursive construction in favor of the fossil fuel industry. Although this was hardly a surprise given opinion columns' role in news reporting, it was concerning that the majority of columns in the commercial media surveyed were written by fossil fuel advocates. Third, the commercial media rejected the notion that many First Nations' resistance to PNW was indicative of extractive sectors' infringement on Indigenous sovereignty and living environment. Instead, many of their reports suggested that the recurring project delays were caused by the "anti-development sentiment" of some Indigenous groups threatened Canada's investment reputation.

In consideration of these features, let us take a closer look at how the commercial media reported PNW from economic, political, and environmental perspectives. To begin with, economic topics were the commercial media's primary concern, and their business sections regularly featured stories discussing the uncertain prospect of PNW in view of changing global LNG market dynamics. Collectively, such stories explicated British Columbia's comparative disadvantages compared to leading players in the global LNG race and cast doubt on the provincial government's promise of a short- to medium-term revenue windfall from LNG export. For example, citing the International Energy Agency's outlook of global LNG market trends, a June 2015 *National Post* report conceded that the intensifying challenges brought by the market downturn had turned LNG exports from BC into a distant prospect:

> In one of the gloomiest forecasts yet for British Columbia's nascent LNG sector, the International Energy Agency says prospects for export projects have "darkened" and deferrals are likely. In a 5 year outlook on global demand for natural gas published Thursday, the Paris-based agency throws cold water on the BC Liberal government's hopes of being home to three

liquefied natural gas projects by 2020. . . . The curtailed outlook reinforces what BC LNG proponents have feared in recent months – that their window of opportunity to build export projects on the West Coast may be closing. As many as 19 consortiums have proposed export projects, but none has taken a final investment decision.

(Hussain, 2015a June 04, para 1–4)

The report continued by noting that falling Japanese LNG prices since 2014 had seriously weakened the economic prospect of projects like PNW. Meanwhile, as global LNG supply was projected to "rise 40 per cent during the next 5 years" (Hussain, 2015a June 04, para 8), British Columbia would be in fierce competition with countries like the United States and Australia. With no operating LNG facility, it had already fallen behind in the race. The combined influence of both factors, the report noted, significantly eroded international investors' confidence. The International Energy Agency's outlook received similar coverage in the *Globe and Mail* (Hume, 2015 June 04) and the *Vancouver Sun* (Penner, 2015 July 2). Later, reports released by energy consultancies such as Wood Mackenzie (Hussain, 2015b September 04) and RS Energy Group (Synder, 2016 October 1) reiterated market changes' persistent damage to BC LNG.

Although these reports by energy analysts represent global energy capital's interest and are dismissive of British Columbia's sociopolitical reality, they offer informative insights into the growing economic challenges confronting energy conglomerates. Yet, such challenges are rarely exposed by Canada's domestic LNG proponents, whose voices dominated the commercial media's business sections. In their narratives, there was a paucity of criticism about the BC Liberal Party's aggressive decision to make LNG its economic priority. Under the "project uncertainty" theme in Table 6.5, only seven commercial media stories problematized British Columbia's excessive policy focus on resource extraction.

Domestic LNG proponents proposed three solutions by which British Columbia could accommodate bleak market realities and high infrastructure costs: (1) streamline the lengthy review process to catch the window of opportunity, (2) offer more incentives to boost foreign investors' attention, or (3) adjust the BC LNG agenda in wait for a future price recovery. When proposing these solutions, they often cited the quick take-off of LNG exports in the United States. For example, a June 2016 opinion piece by National Post's business columnist Claudia Cattaneo accused Canada's lengthy and ineffective regulatory process of making PNW lose contracts to US competitors:

As recently as 3 years ago, Canada was largely viewed as leading the race to export LNG from North America because of its more efficient regulatory process. Then the delays started happening . . . whereas U.S. LNG proponents, already enjoying the advantage of having infrastructure previously built for LNG imports, kept moving forward. In February, Cheniere Energy Inc., using its Sabine Pass facility in Louisiana, was the first U.S. company to ship LNG. The first LNG shipment from Canada is not expected until after 2020.

(Cattaneo, 2016b June 01, para 11–12)

Echoing Cattaneo's attack on Canadian environmental regulation, another notable pro-LNG argument emphasized resource extraction's irreplaceable role in the BC economy, two months before Cattaneo's piece, two senior analysts from the Fraser Institute published an opinion piece in the *Vancouver Sun* which framed PNW's economic benefits as too important to lose:

[The] non-development [of PNW] will come with substantial economic costs. A recent Fraser Institute study found the cost of delay imposed upon LNG investments in BC, defined as export revenues forgone, is substantial at $22.5 billion per year in 2020, rising to $24.8 billion per year in 2025. . . . The National Energy Board's recent Canada's Energy Future 2016 report also shed some light on what LNG means for Canada's natural gas industry. In a scenario where no LNG exports occur between 2015 and 2040, Canadian natural gas production might only experience two per cent growth compared to 19 per cent growth in a scenario with LNG exports.

(Green & Jackson, 2016 April 07, para 6–7)

In sum, LNG proponents' concern over competitiveness aimed at persuading government stakeholders to create a better investment environment through deregulation and subsidy. The absence of any serious inquiry into the boom-and-bust mechanism underlying falling Asian LNG prices reinforced the pro-LNG storyline. The commercial media did not translate energy analysts' warnings about global LNG oversupply into either the narrow concerns over British Columbia's fiscal stability or into broader critiques of neoliberal extractivism's negative socioeconomic impacts. Instead, these warnings were adapted by LNG proponents to demand sustained and coordinated support from the provincial and federal governments to secure shale gas expansion. From a critical perspective, the fundamental goal of such demands for an extractivist state is to covertly increase private capital gain under the guise of public interest.

The commercial media's active defense of extractivism also manifested in their framing of community responses to PNW. In the news sample, the most prevalent opposition claims came from the Lax Kw'alaams First Nation who rejected a $1 billion offer from Petronas in exchange of their consent to locate PNW on Lelu Island, their traditional territory. Before Lax Kw'alaams' high-profile rejection of the PNW offer, several First Nations had already signed LNG benefit agreements, which enabled the BC government to boast about its partnership with Indigenous communities in resource development.

Consequently, when Lax Kw'alaams emerged as a political obstacle, it presented a watershed moment in the disruption of the pro-LNG storyline (Hunter, 2015 May 10).

In response, the commercial media adopted counter-narratives by LNG proponents to undermine the demands of Lax Kw'alaams for Indigenous sovereignty and self-governance. In an opinion piece published shortly after the Lax Kw'alaams rejection, Brian Crowley, who led the conservative think tank Macdonald-Laurier Institute, downplayed the rejection's political implications by suggesting that it signaled merely many Indigenous people's desire for reasoned resource development:

> Those who have concluded from the Lax Kw'alaams' decision on PNW that they are dealing with a people implacably opposed to development . . . missed a different recent announcement by the community. The Lax Kw'alaams have endorsed the Eagle Spirit oil pipeline proposal to bring Alberta oil to the West Coast through their territory. . . . The evidence is that many aboriginal people and communities, including the Lax Kw'alaams, want reasoned development. They need to be clear and consistent in articulating what they want, and governments and project proponents need to get used to the idea that there will be no substitute for respectfully involving aboriginal communities in project planning from the earliest concept stage.
> (Crowley, 2015 May 15, para 9–11)

In line with Crowley's standpoint, the commercial media also published interviews and opinion pieces that framed Lax Kw'alaams as an exceptional case that misrepresented many Indigenous communities' receptive attitudes toward resource extraction. Using their own communities as examples, Indigenous LNG proponents promoted a carefully woven narrative asserting that PNW and other LNG projects would actually function as effective means of reconciliation and empowerment. Although news pieces promoting this narrative were outnumbered by those covering legal challenges and Indigenous protests, their circulation by the commercial media directed public attention to First Nations' internal divisions, thereby underplaying the scope and intensity of local opposition. One prominent Indigenous LNG proponent was Karen Ogen from the First Nations LNG Alliance. In her opinion, the best way for First Nations to fulfill environmental stewardship during resource development was to form partnerships with the state–corporate alliance. As she claimed in an opinion piece appearing in the *Vancouver Sun*:

> While we acknowledge First Nations are stewards of the land, the concern for the environment is widespread among industry proponents and governments as well, and they are doing their due diligence. It is only through participating in the assessment of these projects together that we can ensure the highest environmental standards will be applied. If these

projects proceed, we also must fight to ensure our people have real and meaningful benefits flowing directly to our communities throughout the duration of the projects.

(Ogen, 2016 September 08, para 6)

Claims like Ogen's should be read with caution given their understatement of two important facts. First, Indigenous organizations such as the Union of British Columbia Indian Chiefs and Coastal First Nations were vocal opponents of LNG expansion. Second, the majority of First Nations that signed benefits agreements were small inland bands with limited sources of income and negotiating power. Despite both facts, Indigenous pro-LNG claims remained ideologically compelling since they granted moral legitimization to grassroots LNG supporters, many of whom were laid-off workers with high hopes for the substantial employment boost promised by LNG. Many rural communities' embrace of LNG as a solution to their entrenched poverty formed the populist basis of extractivism, whose voices tended to be amplified by the commercial media.

One notable blind spot in the commercial media's coverage was their failure (or refusal) to address the unity between First Nations and local settler communities in resisting LNG. When environmentalists were quoted, they were represented by either scientists or spokespersons from civil organizations. The perceived liberal elitism underlying these figures allowed LNG proponents to escalate populist attacks on the democratic and normative foundations of environmentalists. For example, an August 2017 opinion piece by Murphy (2017 August 05) made the provocative case that PNW was killed by an "extreme and irrational environmentalism allegedly pervading the BC public sphere".

As shown in Tables 6.5 and 6.6, however, PNW opponents' persistent efforts forced the commercial media to devote considerable attention to the subjects of community opposition and PNW's environmental impacts. The escalating political tension eventually transcended the provincial level in 2016 when the fate of PNW was in the hands of Justin Trudeau's federal government. As the Trudeau government had come into power in 2015 with the promise of reforming the National Energy Board's flawed review process, PNW, as well as other controversial energy projects under review, became a test for Trudeau's climate policies. In January 2016, the Trudeau government disappointed LNG proponents with a new regulation mandating that (1) energy corporations engage in additional consultations with First Nations and (2) new climate tests for proposed energy projects like PNW (McCarthy, 2016 June 25). The regulation led to mixed reactions in the commercial media. Whilst the *Globe and Mail* simply reported it and avoided making overtly negative speculations on PNW, Postmedia sided with LNG advocates and circulated their complaints. Prominent amongst such complaints was the claim that the extension of the review process diminished British Columbia's chance to catch the LNG boat. This claim was in a *National Post* report published on the front page of its March 8 business section. In this feature report, Cattaneo (2016a March 08) – citing an anonymous source from Petronas – suggested that the Petronas-led consortium was losing patience due to its worry that "the [Trudeau] cabinet, which has final say, will keep stalling instead of handing down a decision while the project continues to burn cash . . . and market conditions for LNG are deteriorating" (para 7–8).

The backlash turned out to be unnecessary. Notwithstanding repeated environmental warnings from environmental and Indigenous groups, in September 2017 PNW received conditional approval, which, according to the Trudeau cabinet, came out of thorough consideration of economic and environmental factors. Delighted by this milestone, LNG proponents reversed earlier conservative attacks and spoke highly of the Trudeau government's economic pragmatism. For example, an opinion piece by National Post columnist Michael Den Tandt praised Trudeau's centralist approach to controversial energy projects and even deemed it as a key factor driving the federal Liberals' landslide victory in the 2015 federal election:

> The gambit [of Trudeau's energy strategies] needed to appeal to economic pragmatism. . . . The solution they arrived at was both novel and obvious: cast Justin Trudeau as a champion of resource development, within an environmentalist frame. . . . It worked . . . rather well – until, early in the 2015 federal campaign, Trudeau Co. perceived an even more tantalizing opening in the NDP's pledge of balanced budgets, and zigged sharply to their left, promising deficits and spending.
>
> (Tandt, 2016 September 30, para 3–5)

The ceasefire between LNG proponents and the federal government only lasted for less than a year. Following the cancellation of PNW in July 2017, these proponents returned to their attacks on environmental regulation and declared the balanced approach to the "jobs vs. the environment" conundrum dysfunctional. In an August 2017 opinion piece in the National Post published shortly after PNW's cancellation, former minister of natural resources Joe Oliver accused the Trudeau government of politicizing and delaying the process, which dislodged foreign investors like Petronas:

> When I was minister of natural resources, our Conservative government legislated "one project, one review" in a defined time period, a significant regulatory improvement. Later, we provided an accelerated capital allowance for the project's facilities and extended export licenses. In contrast, the Liberal government denigrated the National Energy Board (NEB), politicized, duplicated and lengthened the consultation and review

processes and broadened their scope. It is now considering the addition of social and cultural impacts, which would exacerbate uncertainty and delay.

(Oliver, 2017 August 2, para 3)

Taken together, the above quotes present a synopsis of the commercial media's shifting attitudes toward Trudeau's energy politics, which, like their coverage of competitiveness, demonstrates the division between government and industry stakeholders. Facing growing political pressure from both conservative and progressive sides, both the Clark and Trudeau governments hewed to a progressive version of extractivism (Pineault, 2016 May 18), with the hope that this balanced approach would reposition Canada as a climate leader whilst simultaneously boosting oil and gas exports. Yet, deteriorating market conditions severely constrained the scope of this policy maneuver.

6.4. Independent Media: No Wealth, No Justice in British Columbia's LNG Fiasco

Despite commercial media's systematic pro-LNG bias, PNW opponents still managed to engage with the public. A key venue for such engagement was independent media the *Tyee* and *Canada's National Observer*, which served as vital communication channels for anti-LNG discourse by privileging and circulating the voices of PNW critics, who were largely marginalized or absent from commercial media. The most novel aspect of both independent media's critical engagement with PNW was the tough questions they raised concerning British Columbia's economic growth path. Although neither of them could compete with commercial media in terms of readership size and publication frequency, their analysis of BC LNG's inherent economic risks outperformed commercial media's blind boosterism of resource extraction. As early as October 2014, an opinion piece by the *Tyee*'s columnist Rafe Mair (who also co-founded the environmental blog *Common Sense Canadian*) warned readers about the exaggeration of LNG's true economic benefits, given the ambiguity surrounding permanent jobs, royalty fees, and taxes:

What are the permanent jobs left over? The evidence is that they will be minimal. . . . What is British Columbia going to make out of this by way of royalty fees and taxes? . . . Companies will resist unto death a tax on the gross profits, meaning that whatever percentage the government and a company agree upon may well be illusory.

(Mair, 2014 October 13, para 14–16)

In July 2015, the Canadian Center for Policy Alternatives (CCPA) released a research report arguing that the BC government intentionally overestimated LNG's job-creation potential. The commercial media downplayed the report by either ignoring it or countering it with rebuttals from prominent government and industry stakeholders (e.g., Jang, 2015 August 06). The *Tyee*, by contrast, recognized the CCPA's warning as part of a growing body of evidence rejecting the business case for BC LNG. It strove to make the case that dissidents of the LNG prosperity rhetoric consisted not only of analysts from progressive civic societies but also government and industry insiders. As Andrew Nikiforuk remarked in a *Tyee* opinion piece:

> When Lee released his findings last year the government immediately attacked the CCPA report as "misguided and poorly researched." A freedom of information request, however, has revealed, once again, that email exchanges between civil servants largely supported Lee's version. One email thread confirms that the Petronas Pacific NorthWest LNG project will launch only "330 long-term operation careers." Clear-headed analyses by the industry around the world also confirm Lee's realistic job assessment and question the government's credibility. The International Monetary Fund, for example, recognizes LNG as a capital-intensive industry with a poor record of job creation.
>
> (Nikiforuk, 2016 March 16)

The principal dispute between the *Tyee* and the commercial media lay in their interpretations of falling LNG prices in Asia. While the *Globe and Mail* and the *National Post* recognized this trend as a market fluctuation, the *Tyee* framed it as a key revelation suggesting that British Columbia had failed in the global LNG race and that the hype surrounding LNG export had turned out to be politically driven exaggeration. Citing Carbon Tracker, a nonprofit group of financial analysts, Nikiforuk (2015a July 22) argued that it makes little economic sense to develop shale gas projects outside of the United States since these projects "need higher prices to be justified, and also that there is Russian gas that is cheaper to supply" (para 9). Likewise, in his opinion piece published by the *Tyee*, Gills (2015 December 21), co-founder of the *Common Sense Canadian* predicted that with the Asian LNG market in freefall with no sign of recovery on the horizon, it would be extremely challenging for the proposed BC LNG projects to break even. In this circumstance, the BC Liberal Party were doomed to break their election promises of LNG-driven prosperity.

Whilst extensively discussing PNW's fragile economic basis, both independent media also offered detailed coverage of PNW's local and global environmental impacts. By doing so, they functioned as intermediaries, assisting the public understanding of complex scientific information. Such coverage frequently quoted environmental experts' dire warnings about PNW at length and then drew upon these warnings to problematize the official environmental assessment of PNW. Consider, for example, their coverage of PNW's threat to the salmon habitat near Lelu Island. In one report on featuring a petition letter penned by ecology scientists and Indigenous leaders from communities throughout the Skeena River watershed, the narrative began with a detailed explanation of why PNW's environmental harm would spread far beyond the mouth of the Skeena River:

> The proposed Pacific Northwest LNG project and related pipelines located at the mouth of the Skeena River in northern British Columbia would affect more than 40 different salmon populations harvested in at least 10 First Nation territories. . . . That is twice the number of First Nations groups that industry proponents identified as needing to be consulted about the impacts of the project. . . . Simon Fraser University professor Jonathan Moore, an aquatic ecologist, explained that "this little local spot [Flora Bank] supports all of these fish from all around," and the LNG terminal could "affect populations of salmon 10 kilometers away or 400 km away in the headwaters."
>
> (Nikiforuk, 2015b August 13, para 1–7)

The narrative continued by elaborating the economic and cultural bonds between the Lax Kw'alaams First Nation and the Skeena River, which added a humanitarian perspective to the abstract scientific findings. Such contextualization also appeared in other environmental stories from the independent media. The commercial media, however, did not adopt this approach and retained a detached language style when reporting PNW-related scientific findings (e.g., Jang, 2015 August 6).

Finally, the most prominent cluster of arguments in both independent media was on political themes, which transformed discussions of PNW's economic and environmental challenges into a radical indictment of the persistent resource-dependency mindset in Canadian economic policymaking. This indictment consists of two key claims. First, British Columbia's pursuit of extractivism violates Indigenous rights and intensifies the social and political injustice already experienced by vulnerable communities. Both independent media did not treat Lax Kw'alaams' struggle against PNW as a mere political spectacle; instead, they contextualized it as exemplary of the existential significance of nature to Indigenous life and culture. Accordingly, their stories on protests against PNW constantly pushed for a broad public conversation on the true meanings of reconciliation and decolonization. The *Tyee*'s report (Gill, 2015 May 9) on why Lax Kw'alaams turned down Petronas's one-billion-plus offer explicitly stressed that many band members felt the risks PNW posed to wild salmon would do irreversible damage to Lax Kw'alaams' ancient customs and endanger their constitutional rights to healthy fish populations. Such concerns were echoed by *Canada's National Observer*. When analyzing the Trudeau government's Indigenous policies, journalist Linnitt

(2016 November 17) provided a strongly worded criticism that the Trudeau government had broken its promise to renew Canada's relationship with Indigenous peoples by allowing controversial projects like PNW to proceed without Indigenous consent.

The second claim concerns the connection between extractivism and government corruption. Both independent media amplified the public concern over oil and gas lobbying and revealed a powerful corporate influence over British Columbia's political system. According to their analyses, fossil fuel cash explains why the provincial government is willing to support a barely profitable shale gas sector with low royalties and taxpayer funded subsidies (Nikiforuk, 2016 March 16). For example, citing research conducted by CCPA, *Canada's National Observer* reviewed policy decisions by the BC Liberal Party in mining, fossil fuels, and climate change and reached the conclusion that these decisions suggested "a pattern of favoritism toward industry that we found increasingly distressing and worthy of much more investigation" (Wood & Hatch, 2017 March 09, para 16). In another collaborative investigation with Discourse Media (Jang, 2017a February 10, 2017b February 13), *Canada's National Observer* expressed its concern that some BC Indigenous chiefs are increasingly part of the corruption scheme, which further weakens Indigenous activism.

6.5. Chapter Conclusion

This chapter provides an in-depth analysis of the coverage of PNW, the now-defunct flagship project of BC LNG, in six Canadian media outlets between September 2014 and August 2017. By tracing how media discourses reacted to the project's rise and fall, I aimed to answer one of the book's central questions: how the competing storylines constructed by pro- and anti-LNG discourse coalitions were reflected in the BC public sphere, as represented by news discourse.

The surveyed public and commercial media framed the PNW controversy primarily in a "jobs versus the environment" dichotomy and, to a lesser extent, a series of divergent views expressed by laid-off workers, Indigenous peoples, and environmental activists. In their discursive sphere, voices addressing how the BC Liberal government's aggressive push for LNG export posed threats to provincial economic health and democratic governance, Indigenous sovereignty, and the environment were generally overwhelmed by those defending LNG's economic and environmental benefits. For readers following LNG news only casually, Canadian mainstream media's framing of LNG was likely to distort their perception of it.

Among the most alarming aspects of Canadian mainstream media's embrace of progressive extractivism is the sense of inevitability they established, which undermines public confidence in economic alternatives to resource development. LNG was framed as the only viable path for strug-gling rural BC communities. This argument was constructed by emphasizing provincial and federal governments' efforts to mitigate local and climate-related environmental impacts: by reinforcing a division between workers and resource-dependent communities on the one hand and LNG critics on the other; by amplifying conservative ideologues' attacks on environmentalism and government regulation; and, finally, by celebrating LNG's regional eco-nomic development as enabling a form of economic reconciliation. Largely concealed, however, were the devastating climate and ecological impacts of large-scale LNG development as well as ongoing violation of Indigenous rights and title to their traditional territories.

Mainstream media's embrace of the progressive extractivism storyline, however, came with two limits: it failed to expose shale gas's fragile economic basis and offer accurate coverage on what mobilized widespread resistance within communities that would be affected by proposed LNG projects. It is possible that independent media could offer better solutions for achieving the normative goal of challenging extractivism's dominance in Canadian policy-making. Previous research (e.g., Gunster, 2011, 2017; Cross et al., 2015) has suggested significant differences between mainstream and independent media, with the latter providing "more optimistic and engaged visions of climate poli-tics than the cynical, pessimistic and largely spectatorial accounts dominating conventional news" (Hackett, 2017, p. 114). The current analysis has further demonstrated independent media's meaningful contributions to environmental reporting. Although low capitalization constrains their access to a broader read-ership, they still managed to outperform mainstream counterparts in providing critical analysis of the limits and inherent risks of LNG and its underlying progressive extractivism. Given commercial media's inherent vulnerability to fossil fuel capital, corporate ownership, and consumerist culture, independent media have the potential to offer crucial space for climate activism.

References

Bennett, W. L. (1996). An introduction to journalism norms and representations of poli-tics. *Political Communication, 13*(4), 373–384. https://doi.org/10.1080/10584609.1 996.9963126

Bickis, I. (2016, August 24). Study casts doubts on environmental benefits of Canadian LNG exports. *CBC News.* www.cbc.ca/news

Cattaneo, C. (2016a, March 8). Petronas losing patience on LNG. *The National Post,* FP1.

Cattaneo, C. (2016b, June 1). Zapped: How Canada's energy patch got scooped by the U.S. *The National Post,* p. A9.

Cross, K., Gunster, S., Piotrowski, M., & Daub, S. (2015). News media and climate politics: Civic engagement and political efficacy in a climate of reluctant cynicism. Canadian Centre for Policy Alternatives. https://www.policyalternatives.ca

Crowley, B. L. (2015, May 15). BC First Nation will accept LNG project – on their terms. *The Globe and Mail* (Breaking News). http://global.factiva.com

Ghoussoub, M. (2017, July 25). Pacific North West LNG project in port Edward, BC, no longer proceeding. *CBC News*. www.cbc.ca

Gill, I. (2015, May 9). No wealth, No justice in $1 billion LNG offer to First Nation band. *The Tyee*. www.thetyee.ca

Gillis, D. (2015, December 21). Three fibs Premier Clark uses to sell LNG dream. *The Tyee*. www.thetyee.ca

Green, K. P., & Jackson, T. (2016, April 07). BC's snoozing while others realize our dream of LNG exports. *The Vancouver Sun*, p. A13.

Gunster, S. (2011). Covering Copenhagen: Climate politics in BC media. Canadian Journal of Communication, 36(3), 477–502. https://doi.org/10.22230/cjc.2011v36n3a2367.

Gunster, S. (2017). Contesting conflict? Efficacy, advocacy and alternative media in British Columbia. In R. A. Hackett, S. Forde, S. Gunster, & K. Foxwell-Norton, Journalism and climate crisis: Public engagement, media alternatives (pp. 120–143). New York, NY: Routledge.

Hackett, R. A. (2017). From frames to paradigms: Civic journalism, peace journalism and alternative media. In R. A. Hackett, S. Forde, S. Gunster, & K. Foxwell-Norton, Journalism and climate crisis: Public engagement, media alternatives (pp. 94-119). New York, NY: Routledge.

Hume, M. (2015, June 04). BC LNG facilities may not be built until after 2020, report says. *The Globe and Mail* (breaking news). http://global.factiva.com

Hunter, J. (2015, May 10). Lacklustre support from BC First Nations signals trouble for LNG facility. *The Globe and Mail* (breaking news). http://global.factiva.com

Hussain, Y. (2015a, June 4). British Columbia's LNG prospects 'darken,' IEA says. *The National Post*, p. FP1.

Hussain, Y. (2015b, September 4). Canada's shot at LNG over: Report; 'Opportunity closed'. *The National Post*, p FP1.

Jang, B. (2015, August 6). BC's LNG project poses threat to salmon habitat Study. *The Globe and Mail* (Breaking News). http://global.factiva.com

Jang, T. (2017a, February 10). Investigation traces flow of public money into hands of BC chiefs in exchange for LNG support. *Canada's National Observer*. www.nationalobserver.com/

Jang, T. (2017b, February 13). BC government scared of 'informed consent' from first nations, says expert. *Canada's National Observer*. www.nationalobserver.com/

Kurjata, A. (2017, July 25). 'I'm scared for my community': Northerners react to cancellation of Pacific North West LNG megaproject. *CBC News*. www.cbc.ca/news

Lax Kw'alaams Band Reject $1B LNG Deal Near Prince Rupert. (2015, May 13). *CBC News*. www.cbc.ca/news

Lelu Island LNG Project Divides First Nations as Protest Continues. (2015, November 12). *CBC News*. www.cbc.ca/news

Linnitt, C. (2016, November 17). After Canada fought for Indigenous rights in the Paris Agreement, what will it do at home? *Canada's National Observer*. www.nationalobserver.com/

Lus, S. (2014, October 06). Petronas LNG: CEO threatens 15-year delay to BC project. CBC News. https://www.cbc.ca/news

Mair, R. (2014, October 13). Four questions about LNG that demand answers. *The Tyee*. www.thetyee.ca

McCarthy, S. (2016, June 25). Ottawa to mandate climate tests for proposed pipelines, LNG terminal. *The Globe and Mail* (Breaking News). http://global.factiva.com

Meuse, M. (2016, October 3). LNG approval shows Trudeau failing Indigenous campaign promises, critics say. *CBC News*. www.cbc.ca/news

Murphy, R. (2017, August 5). The very mean green machine. *The National Post*, p. A13.

Nikiforuk, A. (2015a, July 22). Nine LNG questions for British Columbians to ask their politicians. *The Tyee*. www.thetyee.ca

Nikiforuk, A. (2015b, August 13). LNG project would affect 'grand central station' for Salmon, researchers say. *The Tyee*. www.thetyee.ca

Nikiforuk, A. (2016, March 16). Four more whoppers about LNG in British Columbia. *The Tyee*. www.thetyee.ca

Ogen, K. (2016, September 8). LNG slowdown an opportunity for engagement. *The Vancouver Sun*, p. A16.

Oliver, J. (2017, August 2). Smothering Petronas to death. *The National Post*, FP9.

Penner, D. (2015, July 2). Energy market shift adjusts LNG time frames. *The Vancouver Sun*, p. D1.

Petronas LNG Terminal Set in Salmon's 'Grand Central Station'. (2015, August 07). *CBC News*. www.cbc.ca/news

Pineault, É. (2016, May 18). Welcome to the age of extractivism and extreme oil. *Canada's National Observer*. www.nationalobserver.com

Rich Coleman Pushes for BC's 'Win-Win' $36 billion LNG Project. (2015, July 14). *CBC News*. www.cbc.ca/news

Synder, J. E. (2016, October 1). Petronas assets may be a hard sell: Analyst. *The National Post*, FP2.

Tandt, M. D. (2016, September 30). Template for pipelines: Approval for BC LNG shows liberal strategy. *The National Post*, p. A5.

Tasker, J. P. (2016a, September 27). Federal government approves liquefied natural gas project on BC coast with 190 conditions. *CBC News*. www.cbc.ca

Tasker, J. P. (2016b, September 29). What's next for pacific North West LNG project? 4 questions answered. *CBC News*. www.cbc.ca/news

Wherry, A. (2016, September 28). Trudeau government at pains to explain Pacific Northwest LNG. *CBC News*. www.cbc.ca/news

Wood, L. S., & Hatch, C. (2017, March 9). Time for a corruption inquiry in BC. *Canada's National Observer*. www.nationalobserver.com/

7   Conclusion

As this book began with an anecdote describing how I became interested in the public disputes surrounding over liquefied natural gas (LNG) development in British Columbia (BC), I would like to begin the concluding chapter by reflecting on my own positionality throughout the research and writing process. A substantial portion of the book was written at the Burnaby campus of Simon Fraser University, which is located less than one mile from the tank farm of the controversial Trans Mountain Pipeline expansion project, which is built for transporting Alberta bitumen to an export terminal located in Metro Vancouver. Reading about protests over the pipeline and witnessing them in the neighborhood made me experience extreme carbon less as an object of intellectual inquiry and more as an integral part of my daily life, as did many other Canadians. The book presents a single researcher's analysis of Canada's fossil fuel dilemma, and subtle forms of personal bias are inevitable. In spite of this, it is a sincere effort to address the ambivalent feelings that many Canadians have toward extractive industries, which provide economic benefits to many communities but also substantially increase social and environmental costs.

The book has limitations in its analytical scope. The discursive frames uncovered in the empirical analysis have an exclusive focus on the BC LNG controversy, and I have reservations about their generalizability in other socioeconomic contexts. Accordingly, follow-up research on similar topics could adopt comparative research designs to validate the book's findings. The empirical analysis has mainly relied upon publicly available materials, and thus it would be interesting to conduct follow-up ethnographic studies on BC communities affected by LNG development. Considering the indispensable contributions of First Nations to the anti-LNG discourse coalition and other Canadian environmental movements, it would be worthwhile to conduct additional research on Indigenous politics.

In an era in which climate change has been recognized as a global priority, negotiations and struggles within the discursive sphere of engagement stand out as a prominent frontier of environmental politics. The book acknowledges this trend and offers a timely contribution to the growing body of critical

DOI: 10.4324/9781003350620-7

scholarship on extreme carbon. Shortly, the book concludes by reiterating the key findings and their implications from earlier chapters. Following are my reflections on the theoretical and practical contributions of the case study on BC LNG to the political economy of Canada. I hope to determine, going forwards, what discursive and public mobilization strategies may challenge the entrenched dependency mindset in Canadian policymaking and accelerate the country's transition to a sustainable economy.

7.1. The Emerging Bloc of Progressive Extractivism

The LNG controversy in British Columbia is emblematic of both the ongoing global political struggles over extreme carbon and the current communication barriers against public demands for radical climate change solutions. The rising status of extreme carbon in the global energy landscape suggests the evolving relationship between capital accumulation and carbon-intensive social reproduction, a trending topic in recent energy humanities research. This scholarly trend emerges alongside the growing public awareness that the Anthropocene – the notion that "human activities have shifted from merely influencing the global environment in some ways to dominating it in many ways" (Crutzen & Steffen, 2003, p. 253) – incorrectly placed more emphasis on the expansion of industrialization than the transformation of capitalism (Brevini & Murdock, 2017).

Indeed, as revealed by critical studies of energy transitions (e.g., Mitchell, 2009; Huber, 2013), the expansion of neoliberalism in developed nations since the 1950s has been crucial to the acceleration of climate change. By depicting humanity as a homogenous unit collectively responsible for the acceleration, the Anthropocene conceals humanity's existing internal inequality brought about by commodification, class oppression, and imperialism. According to Moore (2015), instead of the Anthropocene, the "Capitalocene" should be our primary focus.

In response to Moore's call for scholarly attention to the Capitalocene, the first contribution of this book is to explicate the crucial role of communication in legitimizing the ideological underpinnings of capitalism's dependency on fossil fuels. A simple question grounded the book's investigation into the BC LNG controversy: why do government and industry stakeholders tirelessly promote the adoption of extreme carbon like shale gas in social reproduction instead of renewable energy sources? The exploration of this question highlighted the interconnections amongst fossil fuels, capitalism, and communication. In line with extreme carbon controversies elsewhere, the state–industry alliance's pursuit of BC LNG development was fundamentally driven by capitalism's unceasing expansion under the paradigm of petro-market civilization. Just like how coal and oil facilitated the formation of new modes of production under capitalism, the coming of the extreme carbon era marks capitalism's systemic efforts to sustain its energy-intensive forms of social reproduction. The state–industry alliance prefers different forms of extreme carbon over all renewable alternatives since the former poses minimal disturbance to its vested interests in the fossil fuel industry and the global political economy of capitalism.

Thus, although governments and transnational energy conglomerates are increasingly vocal about their awareness of the planetary emergency brought on by climate change, their lack of meaningful action indicates a business-as-usual attitude, which manifested in British Columbia as progressive extractivism – a policy scheme that disguises an extractivist inclination with progressive-sounding rhetoric. Chapter 2 traced the historical roots of progressive extractivism back to the staples bias in Canada's political economy. It argued that Canada's heavy reliance on resource extraction forms a dependency mindset pervading its everyday life and discourse. Also highlighted in the chapter was the similarities between British Columbia's quest for LNG exports and Alberta's reliance on the bitumen industry. Both provinces' political leaders have symbolically blurred the boundary between public interests and the capitalist pressure to extract.

Transnational energy conglomerates' growing interest in shale gas also reflects this extreme carbon's potential to be the dominant energy source in coming decades (Smil, 2015). Throughout the second half of the 20th century, the long-distance transportation of natural gas was bound to underground pipelines due to its physical characteristics, which led to the formation of two separate continental markets: North American and Eurasian. The invention of LNG tankers and other technical improvements enabled profitable transoceanic LNG trade in the early 1960s, and after decades of slow development, global LNG trade eventually surpassed the emerging stage during the first decade of the 21st century. It was the global LNG market's prospect that inspired the BC Liberal Party to put forwards policy initiatives for LNG exports. Chapter 3 reviewed British Columbia's two failed LNG export attempts during the 1980s and 1990s as well as its participation in the frenzy over LNG imports during the 2000s. The review shed light upon the province's enduring fascination towards expanding transpacific trade. Accordingly, the BC LNG controversy should not be interpreted as a simple copycat of public contests over fracking in the United States. It is indicative of an emerging bloc of progressive extractivism built upon Canada's historical and present hinterland status in global capitalism (Pineault, 2018). The complex consists of not only the transnational extractive capital (e.g., energy conglomerates) but also a larger domestic coalition led by centrist/center–left politicians, fossil fuel advocates, and business elites. Resource-dependent workers and their communities form the coalition's popular base.

The identification of Canada's domestic pro-LNG stakeholders complements the existing literature on the media coverage of and public deliberation about fracking. Fracking is an emblematic problem concerning economic growth, environmental protection, and energy transition. The analysis in

Chapters 4 to 6 attended to this controversial extraction method's entire economic linkages. The progressive extractivism storyline constructs a fantasy in which shale gas, as the magic bridge fuel, will direct the world towards a clean future. The most alarming aspect of this storyline lies in its ideological enclosure, which frames extreme carbon dependency as an inevitable aspect of the world's economic future.

The remaining question is whether additional disclosures of the negative environmental impacts of shale gas could save the day. As shown in the divided public opinions on BC LNG, however, regardless of how accurate such disclosures may be, enlisting wider public support beyond a certain threshold proved to be difficult. It is thus insufficient to criticize extractivist narratives without acknowledging the economic sufferings of many resource-dependent communities. Nonetheless, the BC Liberal government's LNG policies still encountered strong public backlash due to regional issues such as economic uncertainty, environmentalism, and Indigenous sovereignty. The discursive dynamics that evoked these issues provide important lessons for the potential of counter narratives in leading to policy change.

7.2. Discursive Contests and Policy Gridlock

The book's next research contribution concerns the blurring of economic and environmental arguments in discursive contests over extreme carbon. The empirical findings in earlier chapters revealed fierce public debates between LNG proponents and opponents on multiple fronts. These debates demonstrated both similarities and differences when compared to fracking controversies in other countries. Similar to other controversies, government and industry stakeholders in British Columbia employed economic narratives to rally public support for LNG development. The extractivist rhetoric embedded in such narratives encountered widespread public concern over LNG's potential environmental impacts.

In terms of differences, however, several key arguments in the BC LNG case complicated the 'jobs versus the environment' dichotomy found in other environmental disputes. Whilst many proponents (especially government stakeholders) devoted concerted efforts to framing shale gas as a clean bridge fuel distinct from dirty coal and crude oil, their counterparts drew on market data from mainstream energy analysts to explicate the fragile economic basis of transpacific LNG trade. To transform traditional environmentally focused communications, these opponents also expanded the scope of their resistance by addressing political issues such as political corruption, local governance, and Indigenous sovereignty. Overall, the differences outweighed the similarities, making BC LNG a unique and insightful case study for comprehending the economic, social, political, and ideological forces underlying the intensifying development of extreme carbon.

The book's application of the argumentative discourse analysis (ADA) framework to the analysis of public discourses about BC LNG exemplifies a comprehensive approach to the study of divergent meanings and the dynamics of competing arguments during policy controversies (Dodge & Lee, 2017; Metze, 2017). The integration of interpretive policy analysis and media effects research into ADA has yielded three interesting findings regarding discourse, ideology, and power.

First, stakeholder communications could lead to shifting and competing policy interpretations even within the same coalition. The detailed account of the pro-LNG discourse coalition in Chapter 4 found conflicting interests and beliefs between government and industry stakeholders. Although both sides agreed upon the rhetorical strategy that frames LNG development as the most ideal solution to much-needed employment growth in rural BC, they were divided on what should be set as the LNG agenda's priorities. Between late 2011 and mid-2014, the BC Liberal government took the lead and constructed a balanced approach to LNG's economic benefits and environmental risks, which enlisted industry stakeholders' positive yet cautious responses.

As Asian natural gas prices began to decline sharply after mid-2014, however, the challenge of profitability emerged and gradually opened a division between government and industry stakeholders, with the latter becoming increasingly dissatisfied with what they deemed as insufficient policy incentives. In subsequent years, the division's escalation was so pronounced that neither the grassroots support mobilized by the 'LNG or bust' frame nor the moral appeal of 'bridge fuel' was able to sustain the pro-LNG storyline's rhetorical strength. The study of inter-stakeholder discursive dynamics suggested how agonistic interactions generate uncertainty and doubt and what influence they exert on policy change (Metze, 2017).

Second, the anti-LNG storyline demonstrated how politics and knowledge production are intertwined in environmental controversies. Although the anti-LNG movement was initiated by environmental arguments, the adverse impacts of fracking, pipelines, and liquefaction plants, the most novel aspect of its storyline is the incorporation of mainstream market analyses, which highlights the growing internal contradictions of petro-market civilization. To date, these contradictions have received limited scholarly attention, and their presence also manifests the idea that discursive (re)production could be both conservative and transformative (Fairclough & Fairclough, 2012). In the current case, economic claims produced by energy market analysts and the opponents' effective communications of them collectively stalled the LNG agenda. Such departure from the conventional 'jobs versus the environment' dichotomy, as pointed out in earlier chapters, invites a reconceptualization of economic knowledge's potential contribution to progressive politics in the era of extreme carbon. Meanwhile, the opponents' discussions about democratic governance and Indigenous sovereignty were equally remarkable given their effective mobilization of concerned citizens via the decolonization and environmental justice frames. These discussions produced new political knowledge about LNG.

Third, the comparative analysis of how different media interacted with the pro- and anti-LNG storylines demonstrated that news reporting actively mediates the consensus, negotiation, gridlock, and polarization between stakeholders. The comparative study of sample media discovered that the news coverage of the Pacific NorthWest LNG project (PNW) underscored three key issues over which inter-storyline contests took shape: (1) the economic and political uncertainties surrounding the project, (2) the public responses to it, and (3) the management of its associated environmental impacts. The discursive boundaries set by these issues provoked interpretive conflicts, which contributed to the policy gridlock between late 2014 and mid-2017. A discourse coalition may break out of the gridlock by resolving existing patterns of polarization in public discourse (Dodge & Lee, 2017). During the BC LNG controversy, however, the pro-LNG discourse coalition failed to do so even with the help of public and commercial media's pro-business agenda. The primary factor leading to this outcome was independent media's contribution to coalition-building amongst LNG opponents. Compared with public and commercial media, the surveyed independent media provided better in-depth analyses revealing the inherent economic risks of LNG exports and the limits of underlying progressive extractivism. Such critical analyses helped to maintain the anti-LNG discourse coalition's momentum over time. As Hackett and his colleagues (2017) note, independent media make meaningful contributions to climate crisis journalism with the provision of counter hegemonic content, public engagement, and political mobilization. The book's findings regarding the unique role of independent media within the anti-LNG discourse coalition support this argument.

7.3. Parting Thoughts: Challenging Extreme Carbon at the Precipice of a Planetary Emergency

Although the book focuses solely on LNG discourses in British Columbia, its findings provide valuable references for examining the rise of fracking controversies in other countries. In Europe and North America, the production of unconventional fossil fuels through fracking has gained significant momentum since the early 2000s. The fossil fuel industry and its proponents often branded unconventional fossil fuels as ideal solutions that simultaneously satisfy global energy demands and facilitate the world's transition towards a low-carbon economy. Such promotional narratives have triggered growing scholarly and public concern.

In a recent review of research on related media coverage, Matthews and Hansen (2018) noted that developing politicization and confrontation inform the news writing about this controversial extraction technique. Typically

found in the mainstream media is a binary construction of hydraulic fracturing, framing it as leading to either economic benefits or environmental
risks. Matthews and Hansen (2018) concluded their review by suggesting
that future research must 'study the activities of various stakeholders that will
drive forward any future coverage [. . .] and widen the focus of its analysis
from studying simple "crisis" moments or high-profile events' (p. 8).

In response to both calls, this book complements the existing energy
communication scholarship by offering a longitudinal study tracing the rise
and fall of the hype over LNG exports in BC. It expands previous analytical frameworks by analyzing both stakeholder communications and media
reports. Its findings shed light on the complex discursive dynamics surrounding the nascent LNG sector in Canada, a country with a dual role in global
extractive chains.

The book's findings also carry practical significance. The heavy blow dealt
by PNW's cancellation did not halt the BC LNG agenda. After forming a
minority government in mid-2017, the center–left BC New Democratic Party
(NDP) inherited the LNG portfolio and continued to negotiate with foreign
investors on remaining LNG proposals. A milestone was achieved on October 1, 2018, when the $40 billion LNG Canada project was approved by its
investors. This became possible only after the BC NDP government made
major concessions, including discounted electricity prices, exemptions from
increases in the BC carbon tax, a corporate income tax break, and a defer-
ral of provincial sales tax on construction (BC Office of the Premier, 2018
March 22). According to Marc Lee (2019), 'the new BC (NDP) government
has offered a much sweeter deal to the LNG industry than what the previous government was willing to extend' (p. 2). At the time of writing (early
2023), both LNG Canada and the previously approved Woodfibre LNG,
after multiple delays, remain under construction, and they continue to face
public opposition. For instance, in January 2020, the hereditary chiefs of the
Wet'suwet'en First Nation led protests against the construction of the Coastal
GasLink Pipeline project (a major component of LNG Canada) across their
traditional territory, which, after being repressed by police, sparked nationwide protests and rallies in solidarity ("Key moments in the Coastal Gas-
Link", 2020 February 11).

Given the pressing need to alter the dominance of extractive capital in
Canada's political economy, it is worthwhile to consider the broader implications of progressive extractivism for the ongoing paradigm shift in Canadian
energy policymaking. When I began researching the BC LNG controversy
in 2015, a widely held opinion among concerned citizens was that Stephen
Harper and his federal Conservative government should be held accountable
for the retreat of environmental regulation. Gutstein (2014) even coined the
term 'Harperism', referring to the Harper administration's neoliberal agenda
as an evolved copy of what Ronald Reagan and Margret Thatcher accom-
plished during the 1980s.

The political backlash against Harperism eventually brought a landslide victory for Justin Trudeau and the federal Liberal Party in the 2015 Canadian federal election. The change in federal leadership, however, has only brought mixed outcomes for Canada's environmentalism since then. Although the Trudeau cabinet has reversed its predecessor's blunt hostility towards environmental protection and climate change, it has also demonstrated unwillingness to shift the Canadian economy away from extreme carbon. As evident in the regulatory review process of PNW, the governments of both Christy Clark and Justin Trudeau worked hand in hand to defend the project's economic necessity and downplay its significant environmental costs.

The provincial and federal policy views on PNW exposed the increasing ambivalence created by progressive extractivism, in which policymakers attempt to legitimize carbon-intensive projects by appropriating progressive talking points. By explicating the discursive strategies employed by LNG proponents, the book enriches comprehension of the state–industry alliance's response to shifting public attitudes toward economic growth and environmental protection I anticipate that the potency of progressive extractivism will further blur the traditional 'jobs versus the environment' dichotomy.

From the perspective of public deliberation, progressive extractivism invites consideration of the abuse of discursive power, which, according to van Dijk (2006), results in 'a form of illegitimate influence by means of discourse in which manipulators make others believe or do things that are in the interest of the manipulator, and against the best interests of the manipulated' (p. 360). Discursive manipulation turns recipients into passive victims instead of active discussion participants. As such, the rhetoric of progressive extractivism is highly problematic since it enables extreme carbon proponents to promote their ideological standpoints via seemingly unproblematic narratives, which maintains existing unsustainable social and economic structures. The rhetoric's ideological enclosure on alternatives to extreme carbon fundamentally weakens the democratic deliberation process. In Canada, the notable trend of media concentration nowadays has further reduced the number of discursive places where meaningful public conversations can occur.

That said, there are still hopes. Progressive extractivism has been criticized by conservative politicians and their supporters due to its notable increase in regulatory cost. Progressive extractivism has encountered a serious crisis, as evidenced by Alberta's growing disagreement with federal environmental policies: a petro-state may abandon it and return to more naked forms of conservative policymaking. This retreat is unquestionably harmful, but its overt inaction on the climate crisis presents an opportunity for public engagement and mobilization on environmental issues.

In addition, progressive extractivism has only been able to enlist limited Indigenous support. During the BC LNG controversy, the determination of some First Nations to reject the infringement on Indigenous rights exerted considerable political pressure on the state–industry alliance and stalled PNW long enough, until its eventual cancellation. Similarly, concerns over Indigenous sovereignty also proved crucial in other successful public struggles against bitumen pipeline expansion in Canada. What becomes clear from these inspiring cases is that many First Nations believe that self-determination and the integrity of their traditional territories, being inseparable components of their Indigenous identity, should never be put on negotiating tables in exchange for economic interests. This belief is also gaining popular support amongst settlers, thanks to gradually improving public conversations over reconciliation and decolonization: citizens are becoming increasingly skeptical of politicians' lip service to reconciliation and sustainability, which are at odds with their actual policymaking practices.

Thus, the formation of an Indigenous–environmental–progressive coalition, which prioritizes the disclosure of extractivism's inherent link with settler colonialism, provides a better alternative to conventional environmental campaigns and the much-needed broad public mobilization to challenge the neoliberal extractivist order. Admittedly, such a coalition could be vulnerable to internal divisions amongst First Nations, which in part results from the state–industry alliance's divide-and-rule tactics as well as the political tension between elected band chiefs and hereditary chiefs under two contrasting modes of governance. Such sociopolitical issues within First Nations are beyond the scope of this book, but one thing is evident: it will be worthwhile for environmentalists to build a stronger alliance with Indigenous activists and to encourage frank conversations about colonialism's enduring impacts in Canada.

Lastly, the most effective arguments by the anti-LNG discourse coalition were directed at LNG projects' inherent economic risks. These economic critiques involved people's lived experiences and desire for employment. Although the mainstream media offered similar reports on the lack of competitiveness in LNG project proposals, they never problematized resource extraction's dominance in Canada's economic policymaking. Thus, further attempts to strengthen the public resistance to extractivism require taking the economy much more seriously. The bridging of economic and ecological risks could serve as a powerful rebuttal to progressive extractivism. However, the opposing viewpoints regarding LNG's precarious economic foundation were largely drowned out by the mainstream media's extensive business updates. They were also short of convincing proposals to address British Columbia's notable urban–rural divide. How to deliver green economy messages beyond the progressive circle remains an acute challenge for environmental communicators.

References

BC Office of the Premier. (2018, March 22). *New framework for natural gas development puts focus on economic and climate targets.* https://news.gov.bc.ca

Brevini, B., & Murdock, G. (2017). Carbon, capitalism, communication. In B. Brevini & G. Murdock (Eds.), *Carbon capitalism and communication* (pp. 1–20). Palgrave Macmillan.

Crutzen, P. J., & Steffen, W. (2003). How long have we been in the Anthropocene era? An editorial comment. *Climatic Change, 61*, 251–257. https://doi.org/10.1023/B:CLIM. 0000004708.74871.62

Dodge, J., & Lee, J. (2017). Framing dynamics and political gridlock: The curious case of hydraulic fracturing in New York. *Journal of Environmental Policy & Planning, 19*(1), 14–34. https://doi.org/10.1080/1523908X.2015.1116378

Fairclough, I., & Fairclough, N. (2012). *Political discourse analysis: A methods for advanced students.* Routledge.

Gutstein, D. (2014). *Harperism: How Stephen Harper and his think tank colleagues have transformed Canada.* James Lorimer & Company.

Hackett, R. A., Forde, S., Gunster, S., & Foxwell-Norton, K. (2017). *Journalism and climate crisis: Public engagement, media alternatives.* Routledge.

Huber, M. (2013). *Lifeblood: Oil, freedom, and the forces of capital.* University of Minnesota Press.

Key Moments in the Coastal GasLink and Wet'suwet'en Conflict: A Timeline. (2020, February 11). *The Toronto Star.* www.thestar.com

Lee, M. (2019, May). *A critical look at British Columbia's new tax breaks and subsidies for LNG.* Canadian Centre for Policy Alternatives. www.policyalternatives.ca

Matthews, J., & Hansen, A. (2018). Fracturing debate? A review of research on media coverage of "fracking". *Frontiers in Communication, 3*, item 41. https://doi. org/10.3389/fcomm.2018.00041

Metze, T. (2017). Fracking the debate: Frame shifts and boundary work in Dutch decision making on shale gas. *Journal of Environmental Policy & Planning, 19*(1), 35–52, https://doi.org/10.1080/1523908X.2014.941462

Mitchell, T. (2009). Carbon democracy. *Economy and Society, 38*(3), 399–432. https://doi.org/10.1080/03085140903020598

Moore, J. W. (2015). *Capitalism in the web of life: Ecology and the accumulation of capital.* Verso.

Pineault, É. (2018). The capitalist pressure to extract: The ecological and political economy of extreme oil in Canada. *Studies in Political Economy, 99*(2), 130–150. https://doi.org/10.1080/07078552.2018.1492063

Smil, V. (2015). *Natural gas: Fuel for the 21st century.* Wiley.

van Dijk, T. (2006). Discourse and manipulation. *Discourse & Society, 17*(3), 359–383. https://doi.org/10.1177/0957926506060250

Index

For Product Safety Concerns and Information please contact our EU
representative GPSR@taylorandfrancis.com
Taylor & Francis Verlag GmbH, Kaufingerstraße 24, 80331 München, Germany